Joyce, Joyceans, and the Rhetoric of Citation

The Florida James Joyce Series

The Florida James Joyce Series
Edited by Zack Bowen

The Autobiographical Novel of Co-Consciousness: Goncharov, Woolf, and Joyce, by Galya Diment (1994)
Bely, Joyce, Döblin: Peripatetics in the City Novel, by Peter I. Barta (1996)
Bloom's Old Sweet Song: Essays on Joyce and Music, by Zack Bowen (1995)
Gender in Joyce, edited by Jolanta W. Wawrzycka and Marlena G. Corcoran (1997)
Greek and Hellenic Culture in Joyce, by R. J. Schork (1998)
Jocoserious Joyce: The Fate of Folly in Ulysses, by Robert H. Bell (paperback edition, 1996)
Joyce, Joyceans, and the Rhetoric of Citation, by Eloise Knowlton (1998)
Joyce and the Jews: Culture and Texts, by Ira B. Nadel (paperback edition, 1996)
Joyce, Milton, and the Theory of Influence, by Patrick Colm Hogan (1995)
Joyce and Popular Culture, edited by R. B. Kershner (1996)
Joyce's Iritis and the Irritated Text: The Dis-lexic Ulysses, by Roy Gottfried (1995)
Joyce's Music and Noise: Theme and Variation in His Writings, by Jack W. Weaver (1998)
Latin and Roman Culture in Joyce, by R. J. Schork (1997)
Narrative Design in Finnegans Wake: *The Wake Lock Picked,* by Harry Burrell (1996)
Reading Joyce Politically, by Trevor L. Williams (1997)
Reauthorizing Joyce, by Vicki Mahaffey (paperback edition, 1995)
Shaw and Joyce: "The Last Word in Stolentelling," by Martha Fodaski Black (1995)

Joyce, Joyceans, and the Rhetoric of Citation

Eloise Knowlton

University Press of Florida
Gainesville Tallahassee Tampa Boca Raton
Pensacola Orlando Miami Jacksonville

Copyright 1998 by the Board of Regents of the State of Florida
Printed in the United States of America on acid-free paper
All rights reserved

03 02 01 00 99 98   6 5 4 3 2 1

Library of Congress Cataloging-in-Publication Data

Knowlton, Eloise.
Joyce, Joyceans, and the rhetoric of citation / by Eloise Knowlton.
p. cm. — (The Florida James Joyce series)
Includes bibliographical references and index.
ISBN 0-8130-1610-X (alk. paper)
1. Joyce, James, 1882-1941—Criticism and interpretation—History. 2. Joyce, James, 1882-1941—Knowledge and learning. 3. Joyce, James, 1882-1941—Technique. 4. Allusions in literature. 5. Narration (Rhetoric). 6. Fiction—Technique. I. Title. II. Series.
PR6019.09Z6767 1998
823'.912—dc21   98-19350

The University Press of Florida is the scholarly publishing agency for the State University System of Florida, comprising Florida A & M University, Florida Atlantic University, Florida International University, Florida State University, University of Central Florida, University of Florida, University of North Florida, University of South Florida, and University of West Florida.

University Press of Florida
15 Northwest 15th Street
Gainesville, FL 32611
http://nersp.nerdc.ufl.edu/~upf

For Eloise Robbins, a most powerful source,
and for Bill Readings, *sine quo non*

Contents

Foreword   ix
Acknowledgments   x

1. *Punctum:* An Introduction   1
   Critical Cartography   3
   On Approach   8
   Coda   10

Part 1: Quotational Foundations

2. Modernity Draws the Line   15
   A Certain History of Quotation   19
   Toward Why   23
   Marking the Quote   25
3. Joyce's Citational Odyssey   35
   Joyce Reads   37
   Dubliners: Reverence, Record, Retribution   39
   A Portrait: The Quoter's Progress   43
   Ulysses: Citation Beside Itself   46

Part 2: Inside the Marks: Implications

4. Self . . . Style. Joyce . . . Author   51
   A Portrait: A Speaking Likeness   53
   The Wizard Endures   62
5. Modern Citation, Modern Historiography   64
   The Past Speaks for Itself   66
   Saying the Same Thing Twice   71
   Joyce and Modernist Citation   73

Part 3: Beyond Quotation: Resistances

6. Moomb   81
   Orality vs. Literacy   86
   Joyce and Oral Sexuality   90

Molly the Mouth   96
7. Joyce and the Joyceans   101
   Against Reading   102
   Under the Influence, Joyce and the Joyceans   106
   Are We Now Postmodern Critics?   112

Notes   115
Bibliography   125
Index   133

Foreword

Knowlton's book deals with textual authority, and especially the rhetoric of quotation in all its forms. The issues treated include such aspects as the nature of written versus oral signification, problems of authorship, fluidity of meaning, feminism, historiography, definitions of modernity, and the way Joyce provides a transition between modernity and postmodernism. No one with a formalist rhetorical perspective on the overarching issues has treated them so extensively in relation to modernism and how it applies to Joyce criticism.

The work is approximately two-thirds theoretical. It deals with the nature of history and its inscription in literature, with particular attention to the actual as reflected in quotations that date and record specific moments of history as quoted from people then living, to be read by readers from another vantage point on the historical continuum. Thus the modernist writer, like Joyce, draws upon the seeming verisimilitude of history, which is interpreted not only by a modern writer to be incorporated into his text with all of its anxiety-of-influence and artistic concerns, but also by contemporary readers with their own mental sets and ambitions.

The study is critically informed by such varied writers as Plato, Kant, Leavis, Foucault, Barthes, Derrida, Irigaray, Bloom, Benstock, and Kenner, presenting the multiple problems every thinking reader encounters in trying to make coherent patterns of the text; and it does so with an ease and seamless understanding of what genuinely matters presented in a language that is clear and precise. Thus quotation becomes metaphorized in its attempts at capturing an actuality both inside and outside a historical context. Besides the insights of the thesis itself, the book provides some remarkable new readings of Joyce's texts involving women.

Zack Bowen
Series Editor

Acknowledgments

The strengths of this work descend to me through others, from whom I now claim a lineage and to whom I refer credit. But how does a critique of quotation give credit where credit is due? Knowing that they are not in themselves the final sources (through Stephen Melville I somehow gain Stanley Cavell as teacher; through Richard Fallis, A. Walton Litz), these were yet the necessary voices.

First and foremost, the late Bill Readings, with whom I worked through the earliest framework of the project, and without whom I could not have begun to speak. This text's strengths derive in large part from the model of his scholarly passion. Next, Richard Fallis, whose acumen, expertise, and confidence in my work kept me going and in useful directions. Then, Stephen Melville, who sees too far for me, and who made me lift my head at important moments. To Karen Lawrence and Jon Stallworthy, encouraging in Sligo and since, and to Barry Knowlton, my in-house classicist, many thanks. Warm gratitude is due to the late Bernard Benstock, whose expert reading helped turn a dissertation inspired by Joyce into a book about him. He was a good sport about chapter 7, too. Zack Bowen saw me through the final revisionary stages with unflagging kindness. Boston University colleagues Robert Wexelblatt, Amy Gottfried, and Sally Sommers Smith offered timely support and advice. Thanks to Gillian Hillis and Susan Fernandez for their friendly and sensitive editing.

A grant from the Vice President for Research and Graduate Studies at Syracuse University and a dissertation fellowship from the same institution funded time to write the first largely theoretical version. The Boston University Humanities Foundation and Dean Brendan Gilbane of Boston University's College of General Studies funded a semester's leave devoted to its Joycean revision and extension. Part of the final chapter exists in another form in "Fending Off the Object: Criticism, Postcriticism, and the Joycean," in *Rereading the New,* ed. Kevin J. H. Dettmar (Ann Arbor: University of Michigan Press, 1992). Translations of Antoine Compagnon's work are my own.

1
Punctum: An Introduction

They ad bîn "provoked" ay ∧ fork, of à grave Brofèsor; àth é's Brèak—fast—table; ;acùtely profèššionally *piquéd,* to=introdùce a notion of time [ùpon à plane (?)sù"fàç'e'] by pùnct! ing oles (sic) in iSpace?!
James Joyce, *Finnegans Wake*

The iconography of the quotation mark unfolds within and around usage: the spur, the scoop, the sperm, the matched and reciprocal symmetry of them, sixty-six and ninety-nine, the yin/yang separated, then doubled. Language hangs on these hooks; hangs together, and hangs separately. Are they two marks, or four, or one? What sum does our pluralization show? Counting will be important here. What inversion of the comma, if these are indeed derived from those available marks of pause, heightened and multiplied? Commas rest the voice; inverted, they exercise it.

They are punctuation, "punctum," the piercing of a surface, violent and violating. Thrust into continuous script, like all punctuation they find their origin in guiding us as we turn dead letters into living speech. Inescapably visual, they signal the return of a perhaps forgotten sound, a dead voice brought back to life, the yearning of the ear beneath the hegemony of the eye.

What does the quotation mark? An insistent separation between you and me, between us and the past. Always this doubleness, always this gap. They mark a certain peculiarly modern separation between reader and what is read, between subject and object, and between reading and writing, where writing counts for more. The quotation marks a nagging worry about telling the truth. (Is this really it, or is this just what somebody said?) A strategy of containment, they attempt to refer words to a stable speaker, who can guarantee them, or be made to take them back.

Joyce never used them, fighting hard to excise those "perverted commas" from his printed works. When Grant Richards, in 1914, finally brought the long and anguished history of *Dubliners*'s publication to a close by offering Joyce a contract, Joyce felt, even in his painfully tenuous position, that he must ask that the quotation mark not be employed in his work. Richards refused, but Joyce's request is significant. Later, from a stronger bargaining position, Joyce made Jonathan Cape reset the whole of the 1924 edition of *A Portrait of the Artist as a Young Man* to remove the inverted commas, saying they "are most unsightly and give an impression of unreality" (R. Ellmann, *James Joyce*, 353). Quotation perverted? Unreal? What reality, what norm is violated? There is more to this than aesthetic preference. Joyce's rejection of the marks signals a wider and deeper rejection of the system they implement: this distinctness, this separation, this orderly containment of language and of us.

Joyce was aware of their origins, with all punctuation, in the medieval *punct*, the pricking of a paper's surface to signal a pause when reading aloud, and the violence inherent in that seemingly neutral practice did not escape him. In ALP's Manifesto (*Finnegans Wake* [hereafter cited as *FW*], 1.5) as the Professor recounts the tale of the Mamafesto, just such a hidden violation, in a documentation of violations, is humorously revealed:

> The unmistaken identity of the persons of the Tiberiast duplex came to light in the most devious of ways. The original document was in what is known as Hanno O'Nonhanno's unbrookable script, that is to say, it showed no signs of punctuation of any sort. Yet on holding the verso against a lit rush this new book of Morses responded most remarkably to the silent query of our world's oldest light and its recto let out the piquant fact that it was but pierced butnot punctured (in the university sense of the term) by numerous stabs and foliated gashes made by a pronged instrument. These paper wounds, four in type, were gradually and correctly understood to mean stop, please stop, do please stop, and O do please stop respectively. (*FW*, 123–44)

In Macbethian fashion, these wounds speak, begging us to stop marking the text with our intention, our separational system, our insistent intelligibility. *Finnegans Wake*'s unbrookability—as with its transgression of so many modern constraints—reveals those mechanisms of control, invisible until offended. We can read in the first professional critical reception of *Finnegans Wake* a prototype of the quotational work modernity applies to textuality at large.

Critical Cartography

Everyone agrees that James Joyce's *Finnegans Wake* is a difficult book. If I quote a piece of it we can easily see its difficulty:

> One cannot even begin to post figure out a statuesquo ante as to how slow in reality the excommunicated Drumcondriac, nate Hamis, really was. Who can say how many pseudostylic shamiana, how few or how many of the most venerated public impostures, how very many piously forged palimpsests slipped in the first place by this morbid process from his pelagiarist pen? (*FW*, 181.34–182.3)

What makes *Finnegans Wake* difficult? One is warned again and again that it is so, most stridently by the voices of its many explicators. A book that requires "skeleton keys" (Campbell and Robinson), "plot summaries" (John Gordon), and "annotations" (Roland McHugh) must be formidable indeed. Anthony Burgess kindly offers us a shorter version, "the gist of the book . . . at least a beginning." (Burgess, vii) Roland McHugh's fulsomely titled *The "Finnegans Wake" Experience* describes one difficulty of reading it—getting to it through the jostling crowd of explicators:

> James Joyce is a fashionable writer and his last book, *Finnegans Wake*, is frequently named in awe and reverence by all kinds of literati. There is a great deal of bluff in this naming, for few prospective readers actually sustain their curiosity for more than a page or two. If they want to know more, they usually turn to guidebooks and commentaries, substituting printed doctrines for direct confrontation with Joyce's text. (McHugh, *Experience*, 1)

It seems odd that McHugh, given this valorization of "direct confrontation," would choose to add to the corpus of "substitutions" by writing not only *The "Finnegans Wake" Experience* but an extensive annotation of the work. However, he goes on to set aside this first difficulty in reading *Finnegans Wake* by attesting anecdotally to the possibility of wresting an "innocent" reading:

> I suppose I have a natural distrust of gurus. I spent almost three years reading *Finnegans Wake* (abbreviated *FW*) before looking at any kind of critical account. I contrived to retain this innocence until I had formulated a coherent system of interpretation. I was then able to evaluate the guidebooks from a neutral vantage point and elude indoctrination. (McHugh, *Experience*, 1)

Leaving aside the difficulty of a "contrived . . . innocence," it seems that to McHugh, at least, the object of the correctly direct and unreductive confrontation with *FW* (he tells us how to reduce it) is to formulate a "coherent system of interpretation," to "evaluate from a neutral vantage point and elude indoctrination." The presumed scientism of this stance means it is no surprise when later, in an autobiographical chapter titled "Learning to Read *Finnegans Wake*," McHugh tells us of his work as a student entymologist, of his growing enthusiasm for reading Joyce's works, and of the similarity in these practices.

> I departed on a university expedition to Western Nigeria to collect acellular slime fungi (Myxomycetes). These are inconspicuous organisms, half plant and half animal, found principally under pieces of water-logged timber on the forest floor. There is a certain parallel between the collection of Myxomycetes and the exegesis of *FW*. In both cases the trick is to acquire an instinct for the potentially most profitable areas to search. . . . Unless you are able to predict whilst upright which sticks will repay your turning them over, you'll wear yourself out on unproductive material. (McHugh, *Experience*, 39)

Leaving aside the difficulty of "acquiring an instinct," we can see that, to McHugh, the reading of *FW* is, like good scientific practice, a question of territory. Apart from finding a way to fend commentators off your ground, the difficulty of reading *FW* is in finding correct locations, scaring out from beneath its Nigerian twigs the acellular fungi of meaning. Once one's ground is chosen and staked, it is simply a matter of sorting out which twigs signify. This impulse to see the reading of *FW* as a territorial problem (the reader in the wilderness) circulates among other commentators, such as Joseph Campbell and H. M. Robinson.

> The vast scope and intricate structure of *Finnegans Wake* gives the book a forbidding aspect of impenetrability. It appears to be a dense and baffling jungle, trackless and overgrown with wanton perversities of form and language. Clearly, such a book is not meant to be idly fingered. It tasks the imagination, exacts discipline and tenacity from those who would march with it. Yet some of the difficulties disappear as soon as the well-disposed reader picks up a few compass clues and gets his bearings. Then the enormous map of *Finnegans Wake* begins slowly to unfold, characters and motifs emerge, themes become recog-

nizable, and Joyce's vocabulary falls more and more familiarly on the accustomed ear. (Campbell and Robinson, 3–4)

Reading *FW*, then, is a project of colonization, of taming a wilderness, of turning a "jungle" into a "map." Of marking off borders. That the text of *FW* resists this kind of separation (in short, is neither plant nor animal) does not ground a reevaluation of the project of taming, but only a sense of greater challenge in doing so, a deeper joy in discovering so lush a subject for critical cartography. Order, imagined in a spatial way, is taken to be findable somewhere among the "trackless and overgrown . . . perversities." If the "disciplined" and "tenacious" reader continues to turn over the right twigs (and reading the text will form you into just such a disciplined and tenacious reader), the recognizable emerges. We will learn discipline in this march.

This economy of difficulty: first of eluding critical incursion, then of controlling the text in order for it to yield the familiar (a familiarity affirmed *before* reading as the true nature of the text itself, as it really is) is the received version of *Finnegans Wake*'s difficulty, a solidly modern version of the readerly. It is a familiar rendition based on a reinscription of the Enlightenment subject, who first cleanses himself of all prejudice then wrestles authentically and alone with a manifestation of nature. Modern readers stand their ground. Remember Immanuel Kant when he writes:

> Enlightenment is man's release from his self-incurred tutelage. Tutelage is man's inability to make use of his understanding without direction from another. Self-incurred is this tutelage when its cause lies not in lack of reason but in lack of resolution and courage to use it without direction from another. *Sapere aude!* "Have courage to use your own reason!"—that is the motto of the Enlightenment. (Kant, 85)

This is a familiar story. Just as our anthologies tell us of the modern necessity to respond to a complex world's complex textuality, the modernist work requires as much work to order and shape both in the writing and in the reading. Our challenge as moderns is to deal with that complexity, to hone it down to meaning: to separate the wheat from the chaff, the quick from the dead. But what of *Finnegans Wake*? Is this its difficulty, that it is all mixed up, that it needs to be separated? Is the difficult experience of reading *Finnegans Wake*, then, the general difficulty of experience, a difficulty by now easily familiar to modern man: to impose meaning on a natural chaos? What textual tool enacts this control, and in what way does *FW* need it? Full of questions, perhaps we should look again at a fragment of the above citation from *FW*:

> One cannot even begin to post figure out a statuesquo ante as to how slow in reality the excommunicated Drumcondriac, nate Hamis, really was. (*FW*, 181.34–36)

First, Campbell and Robinson would hasten to assure us that this passage is part of book 1 (the "Book of the Parents," corresponding to the Viconian Age of Gods, what he called "Theocracy"), chapter 7 (which they title "Shem the Penman" and count as Joyce's last self-portrait). As in *Ulysses*, these divisions are marked in the text not by numbers and titles but by gaps, untitled and unnumbered. By the skeletal efforts of Messrs. Campbell and Robinson, the coordinates of place and location are set. We know where we are by way of cordoning off and setting in relationship discrete sections of *FW*.

We find our way by way of fixing citations (sites). Because we can name a source prior to but proper to the text itself (after all Joyce himself told us of the Viconian correlates, in fact told Samuel Beckett to explain them in *Our Exagmination*) we can return to the text and use the citation to give us "a few compass clues." With one foot placed firmly on the solid ground of the author's intent, we can draw the lines proper to his work. Politeness forbids our questioning why he (Joyce himself) chose to leave them out.

After boning up on Campbell and Robinson's skeleton, Roland McHugh's annotations accompany us onward, into the bush, informing us that "status quo ante bellum" means in Latin "conditions before the war" and that "ante" can also mean "price (from poker)." Also, that "slow" suggests "low" (that quality of Shem the section as a whole is read to elaborate); that Drumcondra is a district of Dublin and that "driac" seems to be formed on the analogy of "hypochondriac." Also that "née" is French for "born" and "Hamis" is Hungarian for "false" or "base." "Hamis" suggests "Ham."

Could the passage now be parsed out? Could it be "translated from dream logic into waking logic," as Campbell and Robinson say is the task confronting the reader of *FW*? Don't we itch to re-say it "in our own words," to impose a clearer and better language on it, as Harry Blamires did for *Ulysses* in his *The Bloomsday Book*? McHugh's annotation might be read as a warning against such a shutting down of signification by way of such a re-saying, were it not for his avowed purpose of helping us, in annotating *FW, learn a language*:

> Reading *Finnegans Wake* is . . . like learning a language: one unconsciously inculcates background material while focussing upon odd nuclei of sense, which are due to aggregate at some future date. (McHugh, *Annotations*, v)

The question for McHugh, Campbell and Robinson, and much *FW* criticism is not one of opening up varied significations, but of widening the territory of a single language, that is, that of *FW*. The difficulty facing us in the reading of *Finnegans Wake* is no less than that of learning the language of languages, a tongue that takes in other languages and incorporates (makes a body of) them. "Provided the reader can repudiate his early assumptions," McHugh assures us, "the *Wake*'s subtle unifiers ought eventually to be discerned" (McHugh, *Annotations*, v). *Finnegans Wake* marks the result of and a return to Proto-Indo-European.

When we add to this claim of textual univocality the traditional notion of a single source for *FW*'s language (it is said to be H.C.E.'s dream, told by one man Joyce) the project of unification is clear. The picture that emerges is one of a single man writing a single voice in a single language that overarches, incorporates, lends order to, a plethora of lesser particulars that are homogenized by virtue of their singleness of source. The modern project of separating, naming, and ordering into a whole is continued in the literary reception of *Finnegans Wake*.

These three necessary modern treatments, then, for *FW*:

1. A bordering off of *FW* from its sources (such as Vico) and its constituent elements (Hungarian, Latin, sections of Dublin).
2. An affirmation of *FW*'s ability to incorporate and control all sources and constituent elements, and to place them in a carefully distinct space *prior* to *FW*. The book's struggle to control sources (at one end) is mirrored in the reader's struggle to fend off received opinion (at the other), but unity and meaning, with effort, emerge for both.
3. An attribution of this textual univocality first to a single character (subject), that is, H.C.E., and ultimately to its author, James Joyce.

Having said this, an answer to the question, "why is *Finnegans Wake* difficult?" seems closer: it needs to be controlled, made into a modern text by a system of separations between its constitutive elements. Quotation structures this specifically modern frame of intelligibility between source and text, between writer and what he reads, with the intent to underpin a univocality and chronological certitude that language—formerly "unbrookable" but now pierced—might be seen to resist. This kind of quotational control becomes clearly visible with a text like *Finnegans Wake*, which so fully rejects it. What is less clearly on view is the way in which the rhetoric of quotation forms and conforms all textuality, and our expectations of ourselves as readers. A weight-bearing pillar of modernity's *episteme*, quotation has a history and enforces an ideology. This work is meant to unearth these, by means of that, eventually, most extraquotational of figures, James Joyce.[1]

On Approach

This approach to Joyce and to quotation derives from the work of Michel Foucault. I imagine myself as continuing, in this history and analysis of quotation, his project of disinterring systems of knowledge and their means of power and control. Quotation, like any system of discourse, exerts power by means of a rhetoric of knowledge, historically accreted and institutionally imbedded. Quotation is a highly literate and institutionally privileged system, a regime to which one must subject oneself in order to be deemed a knower. It is that system that integrates what is known and conditions in what way it is known. Quotation's rules of order pattern the interlacing threads of disciplinary discourse across modern disciplinarity. The implications of what I will trace in literary scholarship extend across the humanities at large. Quotation is a thing all scholars do, the very mark of their scholarliness: historian, classicist, or philosopher. This text's occasional stylistic departures from standard academic form (you have already noted the sentence fragments of the first paragraph) are meant to foster an awareness of disciplinary formation and its conditioning of us all as creatures of the academy.

With Foucault, I begin not with the assumption of some extradiscursive individual, self, author, reader, or authentic work, but with the claim that language constitutes rather than merely describes our ideological and epistemologic horizon. With Foucault, I envision this constitution as a containment and avoidance of certain possibilities in language, for fear of what might happen (to modernity, to us) in the absence of this reliable referent (the quoting subject). Under the umbrella of Foucault's archaeology of discourse, I want to trace what work quotation does for us, and has done to us, and in what way it is a specifically modern means of ordering textuality.

With Foucault, I acknowledge how profoundly disagreeable such an approach is.

I know how irritating it can be to treat discourses in terms not of the gentle, silent, intimate consciousness that is expressed in them, but of an obscure set of anonymous rules. How unpleasant it is to reveal the limitations and necessities of a practice where one is used to seeing, in all its pure transparency, the expression of genius and freedom. How provocative it is to treat as a set of transformations this history of discourses which, until now, has been animated by the reassuring metaphors of life or the intentional continuity of the lived. (Foucault, *Archaeology*, 210)

Beyond Foucault's guiding framework, my most significant source is Antoine Compagnon's *La seconde main: ou le travail de la citation* (1979), the only full-length study of the history and theory of citation extant, and as yet untranslated. Compagnon exposes the origins of quotational control in such a way as to make that control visible. However, in tracing not citation (the more open French term meaning any verbatim repetition) but quotation (the Anglophone term indicating a specific dispensation of repetition), I have read a quotational history inside Compagnon's citational one. Compagnon considers classical usage, where exact reiteration was denigrated along with all mimesis, as a "prehistory" of citation. He sees the Middle Ages, a time of obsessive devotional repetition of scripture, as its apex. In my quotationally informed analysis, the ages of the *poet* and *auctoritas* are similarly premodern modes in that neither participates in quotation's insistent modern liminality. History, for this analysis, falls into modern and extramodern categories, postmodernity reiterating (with a difference) many of premodernity's carelessnesses. My revision of Compagnon's historical schema points up the way in which modern quotation, while clearly broadly modern, has a certain power specific to the Anglo-American world, which may go far to explain why it has not drawn much attention here. Dominance can make for invisibility.

But citation has drawn attention, mostly since the advent of French critical influence. Indeed thinking intertextuality as citation, rather than as quotation, is perhaps the most liberating import of all. Most proximate to this study is Claudette Sartiliot's *Citation and Modernity: Derrida, Joyce, and Brecht,* which I read in 1989 in its first form as a dissertation, and in 1993 in published form. If I found I had to revise Compagnon's citational history to fit what I saw in English usage, I found Sartiliot's work did not historicize the question of citation much at all. (She does not cite Compagnon.) Beyond a brief description of how quotation has become increasingly problematic in the twentieth century (specifically, after Flaubert), Sartiliot focuses exclusively on citation's place in poststructural theory, applying it to modernist literature. (See my review of the book in *The James Joyce Literary Supplement* 8, no. 1 [1994]: 23–24.) Sartiliot and I agree that quotation's reduction to ornament or illustration no longer obtains, but while she takes as given that citation has broken free of the controlling rhetoric of the past, my work means to investigate that past and its means of control, and to question whether citation's modern form—quotation—has indeed passed away.

Joyce, Joyceans, and the Rhetoric of Citation is shaped very like a whale: head and body much unified, and a two-sided tail, somewhat more distinct. Part 1 (a rather large head) tells the story of the rise of the system of quotation, then offers a tour of Joyce's entrance into it. Part 2 (the body continuous) works through Joyce's response to the two primary implications of the quotational regime: the establishment of a modern subject in language, and the organization of modernity's relation to the (texts of the) past. Part 3 (the tail, shorter and rather more pointed) traces more fully some Joyce(an) moments of resistance to the quotational regime: first an erotic orality Joyce associated with women, then the professional Joycean's susceptibility to her object of study.

Coda

So, what is difficult about *Finnegans Wake*? Simply put, it has no quotation marks, no means of bordering one semantic unit from another, one voice from another or one period of history from another. It has no ultimate singular source by which to name and refer it, reliably. It has no narrator, no "author." Joyce said, sitting in a bistro, "This book [Work in Progress] is being written by the people I have met or known" (R. Ellmann, *Joyce*, 6). By then he was all but blind, an "international eyesore," as he called himself, and blind men have trouble seeing territorial boundaries. It is from our necessarily fixed positions as modern (not yet as "postmodern") that we find the textuality of *Finnegans Wake* transgressive, unsettling, *out of control*. The dream of modernity is a dream of solidity, of distinctness, a view of discrete people and things and ideas in a meaningful, organic relationship. Modernity dreams an ordering that unifies multiplicity, incorporates difference, comforts and controls. *Finnegans Wake*, whatever dream it is, is not quite this dream, though Ulyssean efforts have been made to read it as such.

Could we go back to that fragment of *Finnegans Wake*? Could we read it now, ignoring the scientists (just as the scientists have told us to do), instead remembering that Joyce called it music, remembering that Joyce seems to have told Samuel Beckett to warn us about *Finnegans Wake,* that "the danger is in the neatness of identifications," and "Literary criticism is not book-keeping," and "It is not to be read—or rather it is not only to be read" (Beckett, 3). Perhaps one cannot even begin to post figure out a statuesquo ante as to how slow in reality the excommunicated Drumcondriac, nate Hamis, really was. Who can say how many pseudostylic shamiana, how few or how many of the most venerated public impostures, how very many piously forged palimpsests slipped in the first place by this morbid process from his pelagiarist pen?

Part 1

Quotational Foundations

2
Modernity Draws the Line

> When I venture to write indifferently of whatever comes into my head, relying only on my own natural resources, I very often light upon the matter I am trying to deal with in some good author. . . . Then I realize how weak and poor, how heavy and lifeless I am, in comparison with them, and feel pity and contempt for myself.
> Michel de Montaigne, "On the Education of Children"

Modernity has drawn a line. A line around voices. A line under the past. It has circled, encompassed, enclosed voices, in order to separate them, in order to order them, in order to set them one against the other. Here, with Montaigne in the sixteenth century, is depicted a by now familiar struggle, and a struggle that is peculiar to modernity, between the need to speak now and for oneself, and the intimidation, the pressure, the seeming inescapability of the already said. Here, signed by Michel de Montaigne, is the modern struggle to think, to write, somehow authentically. Authentically: that is, as an author, who may discern what counts as "his own" only over and against what is "theirs": the texts of others, the voices of a valued past. Here is a struggle, between a self that must write itself independently, and a force of tradition that is both necessary (as landmark against which the self might be located) and threatening (since this "coincidence," this "following" impinges on the writer's present independence). This contest depends on a structure of separations: between "my" language and "yours," between "my" language and language itself. Here, with Montaigne, is the modern anxiety for separation, identity, and a controlled system of difference.

Modernity has invented a means by which to enact this separation, this bordering of language: quotation. Quotation is a system by which sources and resulting works are kept distinct and brought into relationship as reliably separate entities. Quotation arranges itself in the shape of a debate or dialogue, a confrontation or a joining of corroborative positions. Even when politely invited to speak, a quoted text is never quite at home, must always speak with its host text's interests in mind. Or, conversely, a quotation may so intimidate and overawe an enclosing text as to discredit or supplant its *auth*or*ity*. Quotation divides language, and refers it to individuals who occupy contesting positions. The contest, however, is instituted and ordered between those "individuals," between those positions in language. Quotation understands itself as a fight on the horizontal axis, between presumably distinct subjects, not between the distinctness of those subjects and language itself. Quotation provides that this dynamic may be thought of as a psychologized oepidal drama, anxiety of influence located in an essentialized masculine psyche rather than in a structural dispensation of language.

We might read in a freshman essay, for example, this kind of anxious cordoning at work. The ingenue writer often turns to others' words for sustenance, or protection. Packed with long quotations, such an essay's authorial voice trickles to the margins of the page. Kurt Spellmeyer reads in a student essay (appropriately enough, its topic is suicide) how "the writer attempts to slip, as unobtrusively as possible, out of his text, and out of his own situation, before he has revealed too much of himself."[1] This is precisely the modern writer's situation: to bear the ignominy of comparison with the past, to struggle to assert his own voice, perhaps to find that voice "weak and poor, heavy and lifeless." But to find a voice. To assert an authentic (bordered) subjectivity.

Central to the bordered citational system is its structure of *contestation*. Quotation, when it has not been thought of as supplemental aesthetic ornament, has generally been dismissed as a play of "quotesmanship," matching citations by way of bolstering one or another position in public debate.[2] But what is framed as an add-on, an extra, a supplement to dispute on the level of "individuals," on the level of textuality institutes a formal violence that is not supplementary, but constitutive. This is a matter of property, ownership, and the right to speak. Antoine Compagnon's "inaugural study"[3] of citation describes the effect.

> Ce que les guillemets disent, c'est que la parole est donnée à un autre, que l'auteur se démet de l'énonciation au profit d'un autre: les guillemets designent une re-énonciation, ou un renonciation à un droit d'auteur. Ils font un subtil partage entre sujets, et signalent le lieu ou la silhouette du suject de la citation se profile en retrait, comme un ombre chinoise. (Compagnon, 40)

[Quotation marks indicate that the spoken word is given over to another, that the author turns over enunciation to the profit of another: quotation marks designate a re-enunciation, or a renunciation of the author's rights and royalties. They make a subtle distinction between subjects, and signal the place where the silhouette of the subject of citation is seen in profile, retreating, as in a shadow play.]

But if the author (the citing subject) is seen retreating, it is only in order to give over the stage to another subjectivity, another speaker's rights. The distinction is more than a subtle one, and the figure of the author itself is (at least here) not in question. In handing over the stage, the renouncing author maintains his prestige, in that he has given permission to another. An economy of rights taken or given up, this separation and alternation, rather than inducing the authorial subject to fade to black, instead highlights him and his rights within language.

Likewise, the author may turn his right to speak over to language itself, by placing in quotes that language he must use, but that, he thus indicates, is "not his." A means of both speaking and denying what is spoken, turning it back to language at large, one may separate oneself from one's words by means of these marks. One uses the word, any word, "as it is used," and not, one understands, as one would oneself choose to use it. For lack of a worthier option, the author impresses a word to his service, simultaneously disavowing it. A concession to language, and a means of delimiting that concession, inverted commas used in this fashion maintain that same system of bordering, holding the author somehow in reserve from (his own) language. To mark this word as "theirs" blandly supposes every other word "mine."[4]

This propriety implies a critical control of the quoted discourse, a distanced or ironic use of language one is by means of the inverted comma allowed to disavow and foreground *as* language. Irony, as Kenneth Burke describes it, is the master trope, central to modernity's project of objectivity and crucial within the discourse of modernism. As a means of enacting ironic distancing from the grip of language, the inverted comma constructs a rhetoric whereby the subject stands not only outside THAT language, but outside language itself, entering or retreating "at will." Scare quotes may frighten precisely because, while they seem to offer us distance from and control over ways of talking of which we disapprove ("the language of the marketplace" for Joyce, for instance), they also move us outside of language itself: an impossible space that makes briefly visible our inability really to escape.

The quotational subject's difficult mobility is consonant with quotation's constitutive division between voices. "La friction est une espece de la citation," writes Compagnon, "et la machine a écrire ... [est] un embrayage à friction en perpétuel mouvement" (Compagnon, 43). [Friction is a species of citation, and the typewriter is a perpetual movement of coupling and abrading.] Doubled, inverted, quotation's comma marks an impact, a scraping, a grating of one text against another, of one voice, one subject, one person, against another.[5] Bordered citation is a matter of control, of writers over sources, and of the individual over language. As the place where reading and writing come together (where this friction takes place), we can discern in quotation a deep modern anxiety about control, and about controlling, specifically, one's reading. As a trope of *writers* and what they do, bordered citation suspects reading, rewriting it as a fundamentally *writerly* (active, rigorous, manipulative) practice, where the reader, fending off all but the most consciously controlled influences, writes him*self* in to the field of language. The dominant binary of passivity (associated with reading, "taking in") and activity (associated with writing, with "ex-pressing") has left us unsure of what reading can be. Quotation, governing texts by way of the writerly, represses or ignores reading. It thinks it, to the degree it thinks it at all, either as an incipient stage of writing or as threat and enigma. The "writerliness" of quotation is the mark of this textual control; readerliness has yet to learn to speak, for as soon as it does so, it is written (immediately) into the writerly.[6]

By now, we have begun to suspect much of what modern quotation enacts, though never yet tracing it to this source. Feminisms, Marxisms, deconstruction, psychoanalytic criticism, culture critique, and new historicism in varied and interconnected ways question or reject the humanist individual upheld by modern citational practice: an autonomous, discrete user of language, who is not in turn used (much less *made*) by language. Benjamin Lee Whorf and Edward Sapir suggest language's primacy over the humanist individual's sense of reality in 1921. Emile Benveniste's 1958 "The Subject in Language" points out his internal problematics. In 1966, Roland Barthes pronounces his authorial figuration dead. Michel Foucault helps us think the possibility of his relative newness on the scene of history about the same time. In 1978, Edward Said describes the political hegemony exerted by his scholarly knowledge claims. Ten years later, Wayne Koestenbaum traces the erotics of transgressing this system, when the writer breaks his enforced isolation and collaborates.[7] The quotational subject as a figure of writerly control has been formed as autonomous, male and masterful, and as such is implicated on a broad scale in half a century's critique of logocentrism, phallogocentrism, sexism, racism, and imperialism.

Hazard Adams wrote in 1986 that "Contemporary debate may come to center on the question of whether we really want to dispense with the idea of the individual or the self, as the attack that has occurred in so many quarters on the subject seems to threaten" (Adams, 19). Another decade has hardly seen consensus, though the camps may have solidified. In 1991, Edward Cadava can ask *Who Comes After the Subject?* but an answer remains elusive. Doing away with him seems a dicey business, for even at the point within modernity when he is most resisted—within those intellectualized discourses of modernity's self-critique—he can most firmly abide.[8] Before our critique, or along with our critique of *that* subject, a sense of justice calls us back to read the documents of his construction. Where does the modern individual come from? By what means has he been maintained within and against language? It is this chapter's purpose to trace, within the rhetoric of quotation, one line of descent.

A Certain History of Quotation

"Quotation" is a specifically modern term, entering modern English in 1532 and deriving from the medieval Latin *quotationem,* from the ancient Latin *quotare,* "to count." The Middle English usage, taking its cue from the Latin, meant to count, to mark the number of, as is suggested by a thread of the term's current form, "quota." The first O.E.D. definition for the noun form "quotation" traces its roots in the written: "A (marginal) reference to a passage in a book." It is not until 1646 that quotation as "the action or practice of quoting" has become common enough to be recorded. By 1690 the active, verbal sense has led back to a noun form: "quotation" comes to mean a passage quoted. Ultimately, in the year of Napoleon's push into Russia, the term had taken on a specifically economic usage, meaning the price of stocks or any commodity for sale.

The history of the verb form of the same root "to quote" is similarly caught up in separation, counting, bookishness, and bookkeeping. Its O.E.D. definition lists a progression: "to copy out or repeat a passage or passages from" (1589), "to mark (a book) with numbers (as of chapters, etc.) or with marginal references" (1596), "to give the reference to (a passage in a book" (1651), and "to copy out or repeat (a passage, statement, etc.) from a book, document, speech, etc., with some indication that one is giving the words of another" (1680). Shakespeare's use of the term suggests a variety of senses: (1) identification, naming: "A fellow by the hand of Nature mark'd, Quoted, and sign'd to do a deed of shame" (*King John* 4.2.222); (2) observing, marking: "I am sorry that with better heed and judgement I had not quoted him," (*Hamlet* 2.1.112); (3) holding, containing: "How quote you my folly?" (*Two Gentlemen of Verona* 2.4.18). (Foster, passim) Sir Richard Steele's use of the term one hundred years later demonstrates a slide into the antagonistic: "He shall quote and recite one author against another." The subsequent slippage of the term to indicate the pricing of stock suggests the morphologic company quotation keeps with capitalism.

This very brief etymology broadly traces the node of cultural work done from the sixteenth century onward: from a term used to signify the practice of separation and counting derives a usage of commercial ownership, personal identity, and the tense dynamic of struggle between positions in language. This kind of separation is a particularly modern and a particularly written sense of the relationship between one voice and another. The subject receives his own voice, over and against those of others, and of the past.

Now, this is not to say that there had been no citational practices before 1532, though they were not, I want to claim, quotation. (Most simply, we could say, no one before that year called them "quotation," so they weren't.) Prior, and this meant largely biblical, literacy was meant to record, reference, gloss, and maintain the language of the past, with a concern for keeping distinct who said what.[9] For Compagnon, the tradition of patristic commentary marks an age of the domination of citation, the age of the *auctoritas*, the origin and authority of revelation (Compagnon, 11, 157). Martin Luther's fight was largely a hermeneutic one, whereby what was at issue was whether or in what way the message of the gospels could do anything *but* repeat precisely (that is, precisely as the Church Fathers said it did).[10] But medieval citational practice, far from composing a system of ownership and separation, centered on reverence, continuation, and preservation of prior language: one did not quote with one's own purposes in mind, but rather copied and glossed, by way of preserving intact a train of words that led straight back to God and his Word. In this scheme, the Holy Ghost acts as guarantor for a semantic stability that allows the construction of a "tradition." This is a specifically religious notion of language's power to say the same thing again and again. In the words of the Catholic affirmation of faith, the Holy Spirit is celebrated as he who "has spoken through the prophets." Medieval invocation of prior voices was just that: an invocation, an act of devotion, and precisely not severance and new usage.

The ancient world too had practices of reference to the great words of prior authorities. But while reference to grand predecessors and their ideas was a common, even necessary rhetorical practice for Greek and Roman oratory, here too, the implications of such references must have been quite different from our own. For the Greeks, poetic reuse of received narrative, especially Homer, was the foundation of the theatre and served to unify Attica's diverse elements. The poet was understood to rely not only on his own wit and talent, but on the grace of the muse for inspiration, a "breath from above." The *poet* or "maker" made by way of Homer's inherited opus and divine influence.

At the outset of *The Odyssey,* Homer's invocation indicates (to us) a puzzling subjectival complexity:

> Sing in me, Muse, and through me tell the story / of that man skilled in all ways of contending, / the wanderer, harried for years on end, / after he plundered the stronghold / on the proud height of Troy. (Fitzgerald translation)

At what point does the speaker speak "on his own," and at what point does the muse begin to "sing in him"? Asking to be sung through in order to tell the story, the singer all the same has begun to speak (presumably) without the Muse, and in these few lines has indeed told the story, in concentrated form. These are questions modernity asks; Athens was not concerned with them.

Similarly, Roman practice shared a decentering of the origin of language: the terms classical Latin employs to describe repetition suggest not *separation* but commemoration and continuity of remembrance (*commemorare*), advancing or offering the words of the past (*proferre*), enlarging on a predecessor (*prolatio*), or drawing together with him (*adducere*). Quotare indicated counting, nothing to do with the words of another, or with the words of the past.

Thinking broadly, then, what would now be thought of as "quotesmanship" in ancient texts must be reread. For instance, in the fourth chapter of Matthew (a slightly different version of the episode is found in the fourth chapter of Luke), the "devil cites scripture for his own purpose"[11] from the Ninety-first Psalm, and Jesus responds with words of Mosaic law (Deut. 6:16). This scene can be read as individual discord: as an individualizing contestation. It is indeed a scene of conflict, but is it, precisely, *quotational* conflict? The exchange can instead be read, as Matthew insists again and again we read Jesus' life, as a demonstration of Jesus' fulfillment of the scriptures: his precise repetition marking his bodily manifestation of the Word. It is a particularly *scholarly, written* sensibility that frames the temptation scene in this way, with the reporting of precise words, as if all this existed already, at its moment of enscripture by Matthew, as a written transcript. Even here, the gospeler does not presumably compose this: he records it (though we are told that Jesus was alone with Satan in the wilderness). Note, too, that the citations brought into play do not precisely contradict one another. This seems to be more a matter of finding a guide for present action within Scripture than a matter of "quotesmanship."

This kind of interplay tells us more about the probable state of citational practice for Matthew than it tells us of the very words of Jesus. Matthew felt it wholly appropriate to place the precise words of biblical prophesy in Jesus' mouth. What sense of the truth-value of the verbatim is here? If the words of prophesy can be placed by the chronicler in Jesus' mouth, what kind of history is this? Certainly not the kind of verbatim reporting we now expect from historians, who must quote their sources correctly or face prosecution. This is simply a different kind of citational practice, repetition with a quite different purpose.

The especially Puritan practice, continued until the present day, of scriptural memorization springs from this schism between a premodern and modern notion of the status of the verbatim repetition. One may con over the red-letter version of the Revised Standard Bible in order to learn, presumably, *exactly what Jesus said.* In fact, some Bibles offer nothing but those words, as a kind of excessive realization of the Puritan urge to return to the origin. It is from a post-press trust in the truth-value of the verbatim that such a faith in precise repetition rises. That the recording apostles reconstructed the words of Jesus forty years (at the most proximate) after his death would in itself make problematic such a faith. But that a sense of the truth value of precise repetition did not exist at the time suggests not only the impossibility of *that* kind of authentication of scripture, but also points up the radical problematics of reading the ancients in anything other than a modern manner.

In short, the modern quotational economy is neither that of the Medieval *auctoritas,* the New Testament chronicler, the Roman orator, or the Hellene poet, and a new word, descriptive of a new order of citation, comes into being. What had been repeated, recorded, commemorated, enlarged, and joined up with is now cut off and counted: quoted. An ancient practice of continuity shifts to its precise opposite: separation, discord, and competition. Language becomes a thing one can generate, quantify, commodify, possess, and steal. Shorn from the historicity of language and subjectivity's implication in it, a new quotational economy provides a place for the modern atomistic speaker who speaks and can be held to account for his words.

Toward Why

What forces were at work in this transition? First, the epistemic reconfiguration brought about by moveable type and the ability to reproduce mental work for sale. That language could be efficiently reproduced and sold incited the move toward the commodification of the word. Since along with property comes theft, we might note when the notion of literary looting came to be. "Plagiarism" in the sense of an *intellectual* theft enters the language in 1621, from the older and more general term "plagiary" signifying theft, kidnapping, or—marking the pleasure of transgression—seduction.

The classically condoned Aristotelian principle of imitation, articulated in the *Poetics*—that art imitated nature, and, without shame, other art—was until the seventeenth century the guiding principle of artistic practice. "Something clearly happened in the seventeenth century," writes Thomas Mallon, "something that made the border between necessary imitation and reprehensible replication a much more closely patrolled and perilous ground" (Mallon, 2).

> One thing is clear: plagiarism didn't become a truly sore point with writers until they thought of writing as their trade. Jokes about out-and-out literary theft go back all the way to Aristophanes and *The Frogs*, but what we call plagiarism was more a matter for laughter than litigation. . . . It was printing, of course, that changed everything, putting troubadours out of business and numbering the days when one might circulate a few private, prettily calligraphed copies of one's sonnets or epic. The Writer, a new professional, was invented by a machine. Suddenly his capital and identity were at stake. . . . Eventually a bourgeois world would create its own new genre, the novel, and authors would be brand names, the "new Scott" asked for like this year's carriage model. (Mallon, 3)

The easy modern association between identity and property is traced here. However, Mallon too hastily elides the history of authorial rights. The material claims of the bourgeois author were on the way, pushed on by the press of typescript, but the author was hardly a "sudden" manifestion. It took hard fighting in the eighteenth and nineteenth centuries to establish intellectual work as property proper to a single mind, identifiable with a single source. Now, in the age of the information highway, the battle to define intellectual property rages unabated. Mallon writes, "The inability of the literary and academic worlds adequately to define, much less reasonably punish, instances of plagiarism was something I observed again and again," for "the offense has never lent itself to absolute definition and consensus" (Mallon, xii, 2). Mark Rose agrees, writing, "18th century lawyers sought to fix the notion of literary property, and that project continues today in the vast legal literature devoted to such problems as exactly where to draw the line between idea and expression or exactly how to define the nature of 'fair use'" (Rose, 8). The immensity and extent of copyright and patent law attest to the difficulty of associating a work with a single source, and to the continuing modern necessity to do so. This was a hard-won historical struggle, and a particularly modern one, as we read in Augustine Birrell's *Seven Lectures on the Law and History of Copyright in Books* (1899).

> Whatever charm is possessed by the subject of copyright is largely due to the fact that it is a bundle of ideas and rights of modern origin. It is not like the majority of legal conceptions lost in an antiquity about which we can only guess, and about which each generation guesses differently. . . . But whatever was its origin, the Western World has throughout its long history shown an ever increasing disposition to recognise the right of individuals to the exclusive possession of certain things, and these rights it has clustered together, venerated, worshipped, under the word *property*. (Birrell, 9–11)

The early history of this steady march to uphold the rights of the individual saw royal privilege (permission to print) extended, not to certain authors, who at this time could hardly be said to exist as a profession, but to certain presses and booksellers, who were given exclusive rights to print certain books or certain kinds of books.[12] Royal control was accompanied by church censorship as a way of regulating—but through the presses and booksellers—what should be sold by whom. The shift in where one locates source, from press (machine) to author, is a process that continues well into the twentieth century. Joyce found publishing his works difficult because, under English law, not only the author and publisher, but the pressmen too, were liable if a work was found objectionable.[13] Far more than just "a quirk of the law," as Sally Dennison would have it (80), this is a question of where discourse places origin. Ecclesiastical and secular offenses were traced back not only to authors, but to the machines that reproduced their work, qualifying in an important sense a claim to singular origin. By Joyce's day, modernism's intense commitment to what Margot Norris calls the "heroicized artist" (Norris, *Web*, 8), made for much self-righteous outrage on the part of the avant-garde over this legal stricture. Here, the avant-garde exposes not only its implication in the capitalist systems it often claimed to resist, but its compliance with one of modernity's most totalizing ideological shibboleths. The author's rights demarcate and in significant ways reinforce the bourgeois businessman's. In short, the making of "the author" was both enabled *and* disenabled by the machine that reproduced his work. Despite continued attempts to pin origin to a single person, the medium of reproduction—the press—is never quite invisible. What we read is not, for all the efforts of italic print to suggest it, *his* handwriting.[14]

If the printing press was not a completely faithful advocate of the rise of the author, neither was it the only cultural factor at work to further his emergence. The figure we have inherited clearly paraphrases, as Gilbert and Gubar have argued, the vision of God as (male) creator. One thing we might consider, in order to qualify an exclusively materialist version, is the way in which the notion of the author bears the traces of the seventeenth century's religious transformations. He extends into the interior of our notion of the human those external properties (in both senses) of land, house, and chattel which precede him. The author can be seen as one site of an importation, necessary to the rise of "man," of the dynamics of outer possession to that of inner. This is a suggestively Christian notion, but one dating from a Christianity struggling with the status of the individual, the single human and what is proper to him: a soul, a god. It is only later, and with later interests that St. Augustine's *Confessions* (400 A.D.) is called the first autobiography, the first writing of the self.[15] The Protestant Reformation's insistence on a single and unmediated relationship between text (the gospel) and reader surely prepared the way for the association of the written with an inner singularity, which the economic repercussions companion to the printing press institutionalized, from the outside, into the author. In short, if the printing press made authorship matter materially, the Reformation lent it a spiritual shape.

Marking the Quote

As concern for the ownership of language became a problem in the exterior conditions of the book (copyright laws, the rise of the "author") so it increased as a point of concern within texts themselves. While Latin and Greek texts, devoid of punctuation, were content to mark reported speech with a particularized term to indicate, "He or she said . . . ," there was no system intended to delineate the borders of the interpolated voice. The end was not marked. There was a grammatical shift to indicate reported discourse. M. B. Parkes writes that

> Quotations [in Latin] were introduced by phrases like *scriptum est*, or indicated by *inquit* after a reported statement was placed in the accu-

sative and the verb in the infinitive. *Dicit* was generally reserved for indirect speech where the subject of the reported statement was placed in the accusative case and the verb in the infinitive. (Parkes, 11)

While Parkes distinguishes between direct and indirect discourse, there is no indication that Latin differentiates in anything like this way: indirect reporting and what Parkes calls quotation are treated grammatically, Parkes says, in precisely the same way. Further, that treatment does not award the speaker or writer being represented his own nominative case. The reported discourse remains in the voice of the reporter, which would say, for instance, something like "He said himself to depart," not "He said, 'I'm going out'." It is Parkes's modern, literate sensibility that insists *scriptum est* must have indicated that what follows is understood to be verbatim reporting.

This strongly suggests, then, that classical reported discourse (at least within prose, the medium of "truth") is *indirect* reported discourse, the speaker's paraphrase. There was no visual means by which to punctuate the difference between one speaker's words and another's. While one might trace a text's disposition to something like the *ideas* or the *figures* of the past, this could never be attributed to anything like a relationship traced through *exact words*. We can strengthen statements like Tony Lentz's, that "The ancients were more concerned with accurate reproduction of arguments than with the verbatim recall modern literates associate with recitation" (Lentz, 8), to say that the very distinction between direct and indirect reported speech did not signify in anything like the way it does to literate, post-press modernity.

Antoine Compagnon explains the Platonic/Socratic injunction against direct reported discourse—attempting to represent exactly another's words, or "assuming a voice"—as part of the petty machinery of mimesis. Direct representation of speech was a poetic trick, and had no place either in philosophy or a just state (Compagnon, 102–5). While this injunction is a bit puzzling in a philosophical treatise formed as a directly reported dialogue between speakers, Compagnon suggests that the forbidding of direct reported discourse makes ancient history a "prehistory" of citation, where "precise repetition" was suspect and restricted to the lesser, imitative arts. (With regret, Plato/Socrates dockets Homer among those poets who must be turned out of the republic, even though *The Iliad* serves as an important voice within the *Republic*.)[16]

Trust in exact words is a print-induced value, and is a peculiarly modern thing. Classically, there is simply no such clear delineation between voices within those texts that are thought of, at least in the Platonic vein, as non-fictive, as "true," for there is no textual means of marking it. As Barry Knowlton asks in "Reading the Writing of Speeches" (Knowlton, 7, passim), did Livy's listeners really think he was *quoting* Hannibal's speeches? Could the verbatim have been a criterion for truth to them? Before literacy had fully supplanted orality, there was no such value as the verbatim; to say "he said . . ." is to always recognize that this is *indirect* reported discourse, paraphrase, repeated to the best of the narrator's ability.

No more careful attribution seemed necessary. Ideas or sayings, if attributed at all, were attributed to a great figure of the past by the voice of the speaker. If a grammatical shift occurs to indicate a switch of voice, it is not enough for modern sensibilities: contemporary editors and lexicographers regularly intrude inverted commas back into otherwise carefully exact transcriptions.[17] And all this laxity with regard to who has said precisely what is endemic to orality. In a primarily oral culture, source is not an issue. One always knows who is speaking. In a primarily oral culture, the possibility of the precise reporting of language attached to a single person similarly is not a concern. It is we literate moderns who feel we must make such attributions.[18]

So, with the coming of print, origin becomes more of a problem, and exactitude—because possible now—more of a value. Close on the heels of the press's invention came innovations in typeface that diverged visually from manuscript form. Aldus Manutius the elder (1450–1515) reintroduced Greco-Roman letter forms in his 1494 *De Aetna,* and "modern" typography began to supplant the Gothic print ("black letter") that had retained the look of a hand-copied text. It is with Manutius's invention of italic print, and the Frobens brothers' regularizing it as quotational markers in the first and second decade of the sixteenth century (Parkes, 55), that a means of visually bordering an interpolated text begins. (This was just about the time English began to use the word "quotation" in 1532.) The italic reinvented the direct reporting of speech drama had used all along, and introduced it to legitimate prose, ultimately to become the very sign of that legitimation. To the contemporary intellectual way of thinking, careful citational practices establish one's scholarly credibility.[19]

The italic leads to a subsequent family of textual markers: indentation, dashes, *guillemets, Anfuhrungszeichen,* and inverted commas. This group, all developed and regularized in the seventeenth and eighteenth centuries, were then imported into diverse tongues such as Russian, Chinese, and Japanese, none of which had marked direct speech as such.[20] Italics are the visual mark of a transition of ownership: from the signaling of a sort of general emphasis on words (especially proper names) to the marking of

1. Excerpt from the 1532 edition of Geoffrey Chaucer's *Pardoners Prologue*. Photo courtesy of Syracuse University Arents Special Collection.

direct speech. Rubrication (writing or printing selected words in red) underwent the same shift: from marking emphasis (medieval glossator's practice) to marking the precise utterances of the deity ("Red-Letter" Bibles, nineteenth century).

We may gain a clearer sense of this transition if we review the way reported discourse is represented in a few touchstone first editions. A 1532 edition of Geoffrey Chaucer's *The Pardoners Prologue and Tale* and *The Shypmans Tale* is printed in gothic type, and encloses a "quoth he" or an abbreviated form of it, within parentheses, after the first word of a speech, precisely the formula in Latin (see figure 1). There is no indentation for reported speech: all text extends to the margins of the page, suggestive of a time when parchment and the newfangled British paper were dear. The compositors take special care and extra space to indicate a shift in narrator, shifts that mark the largest sections of the text (*quotare,* to separate texts into sections), and in this we can see a certain nascent stage of concern for the delineation and attribution of language:

> Here endeth the words of the host/and
> here followeth the prologue of
> the Pardoner

Centered and surrounded by white space, the compositors have marked this text into sections based in part on source, but not exclusively: there is a similar break and mark between the Pardoner's prologue and his tale. All reported speech within the bounds of the narrator's voice is, of course, indirect, that is, governed by the narrating voice, without benefit of end bordering, and without the presumption of the verbatim. In short, none of the characters speak for themselves. The narrating voice has an "I," but no one else does.

A 1603 English translation of Montaigne's *Essayes* demonstrates a clear evolution in the handling of reported discourse (see figure 2). The text is set in Roman type, which offers the option of italics, and here a great deal of attention is given to the treatment of citations. Inside this Montaigne, all the bits of the greats: Virgil, Seneca, Catullus, Ovid, if poetry, are both indented *and* italicized. If the citation is prose, it is italicized but not indented, given in the original (usually Latin) followed immediately with the same in English. Also, we catch our first sight of the inverted comma. Here is an example, inset by me within this text, altering the line endings, from Montaigne's "On Prognostications":

> As touching oracles it is very certaine, that
> long before the comming of our sauior

The first Booke. 19

than my writings, if choife may be had in fo worthleffe things. This alfo happeneth vnto me, that where I feeke my felfe, I finde not my felfe: and I finde my felfe more by chaunce, than by the fearch of mine owne judgement. I fhall perhappes have call-forth fome futtle-tie in writing, happily dull and harfh for another, but fmoothe and curious for my felfe. Let vs leave all thefe complements and quaintneffe. That is fpoken by every man, according to his owne ftrength. I have fo loft it, that I wot not what I would have faide, and ftrangers have fometimes found it before me. Had I alwaies a razor about me, where that happneth, I fhould cleane raze my felfe out. Fortune may at fome other time make the light thereof appeare brighter vnto me, than that of mid-day, and will make mee wonder at mine owne faltring or fticking in the myre.

The eleuenth Chapter.

Of Prognoftications.

AS touching Oracles it is very certaine, that long before the comming of our Sauiour Iefus Chrift, they had begunne to loofe their credit: for we fee that *Cicero* laboureth to finde the caufe of their declination: And thefe be his words: *Curifto modo iam oracula Delphis non eduntur non modo noftra atate, fed iamdiu, vt nihil poffit effe contemptius? Why in like forte are not Oracles now vttered, not onely in our times, but a good while fince, fo as now nothing can be more contemptible?* But as for other prognoftikes, that were drawne from the anato-mie of beafts in facrifices, to which *Plato* doth in fome forte afcribe the naturall conftitution of the internall members of them, of the fcraping of chickins, of the flight of birds, *Aues quafdam rerum augurandarum caufas natas effe putamus. We are of opinion, certaine birdes were even bred to prognofticate fome thing of thunders, of turnings and back-recourfe of rivers. Multa cernunt arufpices: multa augures prouident: multa oraculis declarantur: multa vaticinationibus: multa fomnijs: multa portentis.* Soothfayers fee much: bird-prophets fore-fee as much; much is foretold by Oracles; much by prophefies; much by dreames; much by portentuous fignes, and others, vpon which antiquitie grounded moft of their enterprifes, as well publike as private: our religion hath abolifhed them. And albeit there remaine yet amongft vs fome meanes of divination in the ftarres, in fpirits, in fhapes of the body, in dreames, and elfewhere a notable example of the mad and fond curiofitie of our nature, ammufing it felfe to preoccupate future things, as if it had not enough to digeft the prefent.

Ck.diuin.lib.2

Lucan.lib.2 4.

————cur hanc tibi rector Olympi
Sollicitis vifum mortalibus addere curam,
Nofcant venturas vt dira per omnia clades!
Sit fubitum quodcunque paras fit caeca futuri
Mens hominum fati, ficeat fperare timenti.
Why pleas'd it thee, thou ruler of the fpheares,
To adde this care to mortalls care-clog'd minde,
That they their miferie know, ere it appeares?
Let thy drifts fodaine come; let men be blinde
T'wards future fate: oh let him hope that feares.

Ne vtile quidem eft fcire quid futurum fit: Miferum eft enim nihil proficientem angi. It is not fo much as profitable for vs, to know what is to come, for it is a miferable thing, a man fhould fret and be vexed, and doe no good. Yet is it of much leffe authoritie, loe here wherefore the example of *Francis Marquis* of *Saluzzo* hath feemed remarkeable vnto me: who being Lieutenant Generall vnto *Francis* our King, and over all his forces, which hee then had beyond the Mountaines in *Italie*, a man highly favoured in all our court, and otherwife infinitely behold-ing to the King for his owne Marquifate, which his brother had forfeited: and having no occafion to doe it, yea and his minde and affections contradicting the fame, fuffered himfelfe to be frighted and deluded (as it hath fince been manifeftly prooved) by the fond prognofticuations, which then throughout all *Europe* were given out to the advantage of the Emperor

C 4

2. Excerpt from the 1603 edition of Michel de Montaigne's *Essaies*. Photo courtesy of Syracuse University Arents Special Collection.

> *Iesus Christ,* they had begunne to loose their
> credit: for wee see that *Cicero* laboreth to find
> the cause of their declination: and these be his
> words: *cur isto modo iam oracula delphis non* "
> *eduntur non modo nostra aetate, sediamdiu, ut* "
> *nihil possit ess contemptus? Why in like sort* "
> *are not oracles uttered, not onely in our own* "
> *times, but goodwhile since, so as now nothing* "
> *can be more contemptible?* "

This is quotation worthy of the name. It is marked carefully, bordered throughout by virtue of the italic, a distinction intensified by the marginal inverted commas (at this stage, when used at all, placed in the *outside* margin of a page). The quotation speaks in its own nominative case: it is a separate subject from its quoter, Montaigne. We slowly begin to see inverted commas moving inside the text itself, eventually to displace the italic. Montaigne's effort to border this quote, ("and these be his words") has been materially augmented, indeed *enacted,* by the new visual disposition of the words on the page. It is not until the early nineteenth century that indention and the quotation mark's head and foot useage is regularized. An 1813 grammar guide states the rule much as it stands today, though deviating wildly in its own quotational practices.[21]

What the return of direct reported speech means is a new choice for prose writers: whether to speak for others, or to allow others to speak for themselves. Increasingly, letting them speak for themselves signals believability. We can read a certain quivering in the treatment of reported discourse in a first edition of John Milton's 1670 *History of Britain* (see figure 3). Here is a passage describing part of the story of King Lear:

> *Gonerill* th' Eldest apprehending too well her Fathers weakness, makes answer invoking Heav'n, That *she loved him above her soul. Therefore,* quoth the old man overjoy'd, *since thou so honourst my declin'd Age, to thee and the Husband whom thou shalt choose, I give the third part of my Realm.*

Despite the italic print for Gonerill's words, the grammar has not shifted to accommodate her: she remains in the third person, depicted from the standpoint of the bounding authorial voice. Lear, on the other hand, has an "I"; the grammar shifts to the first person for him, and he gets much the longest speech. While this kind of treatment of reported speech dramatizes well a certain gender discrepancy (men speak; women are spoken for) that might

> Book I.   *The History of* England.   17
> *Paladur*, now *Septonia* or *Shaftsbury:* but this by others is contradicted.
>   *Bladud* his Son built *Caerbadus* or *Bathe*, and those medcinable Waters he dedicated to *Minerva*, in whose Temple there he kept fire continually burning. He was a man of great invention, and taught Necromancie: till having made him Wings to fly, he fell down upon the Temple of *Apollo* in *Trinovant*, and so dy'd after twenty years Reigne.
>   Hitherto from Father to Son the direct Line hath run on: but *Leir* who next Reign'd, had only three Daughters, and no Male Issue: govern'd laudably, and built *Caer-Leir*, now *Leicestre*, on the Bank of *Sora*. But at last, failing through Age, he determines to bestow his Daughters, and so among them to divide his Kingdom. Yet first to try which of them lov'd him best (a Trial that might have made him, had he known as wisely how to try, as he seem'd to know how much the trying behoov'd him) *he resolves a simple resolution, to ask them solemly in order; and which of them should profess largest, her to beleev.* *Gonorill* th' Eldest apprehending too well her Fathers weakness, makes answer invoking Heav'n, *That she lov'd him above her Soul*. Therfore, quoth the old man overjoy'd, *since thou so honour'st my declin'd Age, to thee and the Husband whom thou shalt choose, I give the third part of my Realm*. So fair a speeding for a few words soon utter'd, was to *Regan* the second, ample instruction what to say. She on the same demand spares no protesting, and the Gods must witness, that otherwise to express her thoughts she knew not, but that *she lov'd him above all Creatures*; and so receavs an equal reward with her Sister. But *Cordelia* the youngest, though hitherto best belov'd, and now before her Eyes the
>   D   rich

3. Excerpt from the 1670 edition of John Milton's *History of Britain*. Photo courtesy of Syracuse University Arents Special Collection.

be traced on a larger scale, the point here is that there were two options open to Milton in a way that there could not have been before the invention of the print clarity of the italic, and, ultimately, of the inverted comma. Italics made tenser the status of who is saying what, what words belong to whom, and whether or not language can be rightly attributed.

What this brief review of the evolution of bordered citation suggests, then, is a slow, print-driven shift, from oral culture's indirect speech—where reported speech amounts to paraphrase, without a sense of effacing or falsifying the past—to modern literate direct reported speech. This marks a vast alteration in our sense of the intersection between a speaking subject and the past. What classical and medieval textuality took as given—a continuity with a person and a past that can be commemorated and added on to—modernity struggles to *quote,* that is, cut off from the past in its verbatim form, not to represent, but to re-present to the present: a strange but authentic artifact, a real, speaking person from a remote but recoverable past.

That the first printerly medium of the quote—the italic—sought to suggest the living hand of manuscript within the seemingly inhuman perfection of Roman typeface, and that it was used to indicate first and foremost proper names and the words attached to them, points up the anxiety of an oral culture, where source is never at issue, to come to terms with a writtenness that effaces the person behind the words, detaches sources from their products, and replaces familiar speakers with removed authors. Restoring a talking subject to the frame of the written, quotation is a modern compensation for the loss of the personal, an attempt not only to make sources of words again proximate, but to do the same for a past that writing would seem to make impenetrable and lost. Bordered modern citation, quotation and its variant forms, do not quote specific words so much as they quote a personal self in a reachable past.

With modern bordered citation, language gets attached to particular, isolated subjects who are presumed to be its origin and source: to preexist it. These now isolated subjects are cut off not only from the communal implications of prequotational language (where speakers add on to language, rather than make their own) but from a continuous, everywhere-available past such a language would provide. Torn from a language that might ground his communality, the quoter goes his solitary way, a different kind of speaker, a different kind of self.

Now, the pressure to establish one's difference by way of language builds, and style begins to make the man. James Joyce, deferred thoughout this chapter, beings to loom on our horizon: an author, a writer, just such a solitary exile. Entering this historical trace from its center (a rigorously correct Jesuit education) and from its margin (a still strongly oral Ireland, a transgressive avant-garde), Joyce's increasingly experimental works move among and ultimately beyond this system of control, foregrounding in his transgression its hold on the reading and writing mind. Chapter three, "Joyce's Citational Odyssey," will follow out Joyce's journey into the quotational regime.

3

Joyce's Citational Odyssey

—In short, a complex personality, an enigma, a contradictory spokesman for the truth, an obsessive litigant and yet an essentially private man who wished his total indifference to public notice to be universally recognised —in short, a liar and a hypocrite, a tight-fisted, sponging, fornicating drunk.

Henry Carr in Tom Stoppard's *Travesties*

It might be said that Joyce criticism from the start has been preoccupied with Joyce as a lawbreaker, an apostate, and a rebel, with earlier work exploring the rebellion *in* his works (as a theme) and later criticism exploring the rebellion *of* his works (as a textual resistance). Early, and enduringly, Joyce is a "revolutionary" (Jolas, 1929; MacCabe, 1978), then an "alien," if a "sympathetic" one (Morse, 1959); now he is "illicit" and "postmodern" (Dettmar, 1996).[1]

If quotation is a law, what was Joyce's relation to law?[2] As we might suppose, complex. In his youth, and through his doppelgänger Stephen Dedalus, Joyce grandly rejected various systems of legal control: property (he claimed to be a socialist and spent wildly whatever he earned or borrowed), marriage (he did not offer Nora Barnacle marriage when he invited her to flee Ireland with him), citizenship (he left Ireland in 1904 and wandered through Europe), religion (he rejected first the priesthood, then the Roman Catholic Church). For Joyce, even paternity was a "legal fiction," exposing patriarchy and law as equally oppressive, contingent and constructed.

Nevertheless, Joyce's resistance to legal systems did not preclude his energetic litigiousness over what may seem to us now astonishing trivial issues: Henry Carr's name-calling? The price of a few theater tickets? (R. Ellmann, *Joyce*, 426–28). His rejection of marriage did not preclude his living monogamously, eventually marrying Nora Barnacle in 1931 so that his children and grandson might inherit his property, not in their own names, but explicitly *as his children*. The legal fictiveness of his paternity did not preclude his insistence on it.³ Rejection of Catholicism did not preclude an occasional visit to Mass, and now, with European unity advancing, even nationality might be said, in a way, to be catching up with Joyce, the quintessential European.

About authorial rights the record is equally contradictory. In calling himself a "scissors and paste man" (R. Ellmann, *Joyce,* 626), in many, many jokes about plagiarism, in comparing himself to his own disadvantage with Yeats's imaginative originality (661n), Joyce locates his work among the found objects of language, not, or not purely, in himself: "Chance furnishes me with what I need. I'm like a man who stumbles: my foot strikes something, I look down, and there is exactly what I'm in need of" (661n).

Richard Ellmann's biography of Joyce layers a romantic notion of authorial imagination over these admissions, writing, "His method of composition was . . . the imaginative absorption of stray material. The method did not please Joyce very much because he considered it not imaginative enough, but it was the only way he could work" (250). "Imaginative absorption" places the emphasis first on Joyce's imagination, while what is absorbed is clearly Joyce's sources, not Joyce himself. Yet this was the Joyce who would write to Nora Barnacle, "I know and feel that if I am to write anything fine or noble in the future I shall do so only by listening at the doors of your heart" (quoted in Ellmann, 304–5). This was the Joyce who would write to Harriet Weaver, "My head is full of pebbles and broken matches and bits of glass picked up 'most everywhere" (quoted in Ellmann, 512).

But having listened, and having written, Joyce was quick to claim his work as his own. When Samuel Roth pirated *Ulysses,* Joyce quickly sued, and generated an international petition condemning Roth for making money off someone else's words (R. Ellmann, *Joyce,* 585–87). When in 1931 the *Frankfurter Zeitung* published a story by "James Joyce," Joyce leapt to institute proceedings for forgery. The paper printed a retraction explaining that the translator had mistakenly substituted "James" for "Michael," the actual author. Joyce received letters of apology from Michael Joyce and the translator, as well as the retraction, but only grudgingly dropped the case (639–40). Joyce's grandson Stephen James Joyce, a strong advocate of Joyce's (and Joyces') property rights, when confronted with this contradiction as "hypocrisy," replied, "We live in an age of hypocrisy."⁴ Rather than try to catch Joyce out in these kinds of inconsistencies—

not a particularly illuminating task—I'd rather trace his citational trajectory: his odyssey into and away from quotational propriety. To begin at the beginning, Joyce reads.

Joyce Reads

Joyce is in bed. It is mid-morning, and the house is noisy and chaotic. The family's voices are never inaudible, the children are around, the window is open and voices in the street intertwine with those inside. Joyce reads: Homer, Newman, Ibsen, Nietzsche, Vico. He reads so widely that "it is hard to say definitely of any important creative work published in the late nineteenth century that Joyce had not read it" (R. Ellmann, *Joyce*, 75). To this canonical syllabus we can add the massive body of popular literature Joyce took in: the "newspapers, magazines, romances, 'self-improvement' guides, and casual works of fiction that lie scattered throughout the text" (Kershner, 2). Everything Joyce reads is up for grabs, for critique or for mutation. Everything he reads, just as everything he experiences, is grist for his mill, ripe for the picking. The more he admires what he reads, the more it will color or structure his own, new text. For Joyce, literature is always in the making.

Appropriation comes easily to Joyce, with his astonishing memory for verbatim prose—he can recite pages at a stretch—and his keen ear for distinctive rhetoric. A certain Irish tradition of domestic performance instills in him a repertory spirit. No sense of undue propriety or piety restrains his taking whatever he wants, turning it to his own uses. Ransacking Catholic theology, the young Joyce transforms Thomas Aquinas, the central figure in the ethical structure of Catholicism, into an aesthete. He borrows (without returning it) that sacred Christian term *epiphany*, the revelation of the godhead, and employs it to mark tawdry moments of everyday life. Parnell and Jesus will be made to serve his purposes of self-definition, his very use of them constituting liberation from political or religious commitment. Later, *The Odyssey*, *The New Science*, and a thousand others will be made to serve his ends. At play among the stacks, Joyce enacts a gleeful and utterly rapacious dismemberment of the texts and figures of the past. Joyce's attitude toward books will mirror his attitude toward people: they exist to serve him in his writerly quest. Joyce saw his father buy him books while the family went hungry (R. Ellmann, *Joyce*, 75). Perhaps he took his cue from that, both in his notion of himself as a privileged reader and in a certain long-standing equation of books and food as equally edible.

Joyce's art, as André Topia says, quoting Foucault on Flaubert, "arises with the birth of the archives" (quoted in Topia, 103). But if Joyce is born in the archives, it is a bloody birth. Now, Aquinas, Parnell, Jesus are never without Joyce's treatment of them. One story can give us a view of this James Joyce. Ellmann tells of a 1902 Paris meeting between Joyce and John Synge, during which Joyce disparaged Synge's *Riders to the Sea* as insufficiently Aristotelian. Since Joyce would later translate the play and had already committed some of its speeches to memory, Ellmann is puzzled by Joyce's aggressive dismissal. Even more strangely, Joyce then shares with Synge an odd little book:

> Joyce showed Synge a notebook containing *Memorabilia,* which turned out to be merely solecisms by contemporaries.... Synge was annoyed, pushed the book aside, and said, "What of it? It is not important at all." He found Joyce obsessed by rules. (R. Ellmann, 124–25)

Well might Synge find Joyce "obsessed by rules," but there is more at work here than neurotic nit-picking. With his nasty notebook of quotes, with his mean-spirited disparagement of Synge via Aristotle, Joyce acts in the purest tradition of quotation: one quotes to control, to establish identity and dominance over others' words, over others. James Joyce, the yet-unmade writer, confronted with a John Synge and with his own admiration for *Riders*, asserts his primacy over both by way of quotation, a rhetoric of retention and reuse. Joyce told Arthur Power that the acid test for any work is to copy it out. Such a practice made for "disastrous revelations"[5] (Ellmann, 609n).

All the better to perform this maneuver on one's contemporaries, deploying against them a literary tradition Joyce thereby claims as his heritage, his legitimation, though he will supersede it, too. Synge is insufficiently Aristotelian, which is to say, outside of the line of descent. The *Poetics*, itself comprised of fragments cobbled together after Aristotle's death, works to split and diminish *Riders to the Sea*. *Memorabilia,* a sort of anti-Bartlett's—not respect but ridicule—provides Joyce with the power to speak, over and against others and over and against the medium of writing itself: language. Joyce the quoter has superseded these words, captured in his repetition their inherent weakness and his now established dominance.

This quotational mastery lies at the heart not only of Joyce's early perception of his writing, but of Joyce's scholarly reception. Taking their cue from Joyce, but more broadly from the system of quotation at large, Joyceans see in Joyce's work the transmogrification of the found, the collection and recontextualization of the received. "Have you ever noticed," Joyce crowed to Frank Budgen, "when you get an idea, how much I can make of it?" (Ellmann, 439) Joyce's work is radically quotational, in that it performs this kind of transubstantiation before our very eyes, by means of a repetition followed by a registering of new meaning for the interpolation in its new context. We are meant to see both the origin text and its overcoming.

Joyce's work and its critical scholarship are fully continuous in this power and pleasure: that one can demonstrate dominance and enact change by means of (this kind of) citation. And this is no doubt one reason why Joyce has so very, very, many critical readers. When a Joyce scholar quotes Joyce, he or she replicates within the carefully controlled discourse of scholarly quotation what the Joyce text enacts in a progressively less contained way: the capture and control of a past and an other. Interjected into scholarly discourse, a Joyce quote (particularly from the later works) has the effect of a fun-house mirror, returning an image of quotational appropriation that skews and exaggerates it.

Joyce quit writing criticism, that most correct of quotational genres, early on. His first publication, a review essay of Ibsen's *When We Dead Awaken* did not lead to many others; his intermittent excursions into lecturing were perfunctory. Synge's assessment to Augusta Gregory, based on that Paris meeting, that if Joyce could avoid insanity, he might "do excellent essay-writing" (Ellmann, 125n), would not be realized. Joyce quickly moved beyond the propriety (and pettiness) of *Memorabilia* to craft a new notion of citation and to found a far richer relation with his reading, a relation that would work itself out in the unbounded pages of fictional discourse.

He would never leave behind, however, the aura of the master who masters, precisely, the whole of the literary tradition and its medium in language. Writing, after Joyce, will become far harder, so powerfully has he remade the canon. He is the one who, Eliot said, had "killed the nineteenth century, exposed the futility of all styles" (Ellmann, 528). He is the one who will "halt female pens" (Scott, 145). He is the one who said, and who is remembered for having said, "*Je suis au bout de l'anglais*" [I am at the end of English] (Ellmann, 546).

Dubliners: Reverence, Record, Retribution

Seen swiftly, and from a great height, the Joyce canon moves from a conventional observance of quotational propriety to its fullest explosion in *Finnegans Wake*. *Dubliners*, while by no means leaving aside the role of reading in the lives of its subjects (see Brandon Kershner's tracing of it in *Joyce, Bakhtin, and Popular Literature*), nevertheless foregrounds this readerly influence most fully as a theme within an authorial discourse that (for now) remains (ostensibly) proof against books. Joyce's Ibsenian "lofty, impersonal power" may have been guided by Ibsen's prose, but Ibsen stays at a stable remove. Joyce's early realist work processes Joyce's past into fiction; later, Joyce's writing will process not "real life," but real words, making the relation between these increasingly problematic.

Within this properly stable narrating voice, and by its means, Joyce investigates the dynamics of reiteration available to him. "The Sisters" reflects Joyce's understanding of the quotational history I have outlined above. One can read (repeat) as an *auctoritas,* as a spiritualized conduit of divine revelation, to invoke and commemorate, in short, to pray. One can read (that is, repeat) to allow the tradition to reveal itself. Or one may read with one's own interests in mind, holding the text at arm's length, manipulating and molding it. "The Sisters" sets *auctoritas* against author.

At the outset of the collection, Father Flynn has initiated the boy of "The Sisters" into the world of books as an *auctoritas,* reading as religion, repetition of precise words a holy duty, a means of revelation, a tie to tradition. This is the Catholic Ireland of catechism, mass, breviary, and rosary: one repeats those words again and again and again, and they mean the same thing every time, a meaning God has granted them. One memorizes, one reiterates, one carries on the Word. Flynn sets him to reciting the responses of the Mass "which he had made me learn by heart" (12).

Flynn's scholarly credentials clearly derive from this medieval readerly tradition: "He had studied in the Irish college in Rome and he taught me to pronounce Latin properly" (11). The boy is awestruck by this world of big books ("the fathers of the Church had written books as thick as the *Post Office Directory* and as closely printed as the law notices in the newspaper" [11]), but their contents are still a mystery to him: it is their heft—their massive size, age, and authority—that impresses. The boy does not read them: the priest will reiterate their meaning to him.

The hermeneutic itch—the promise of secrets revealed—characterizes this literacy. The ordained priest, understood through apostolic succession to be continuous with Jesus and with his meaning, can disclose the secrets of the Church, which are the secrets of the divine word, immanent within language, and untouched by human use of it: a very pure form of logocentrism. For the boy, Flynn unearths mysteries:

> He told me stories about the catacombs and about Napoleon Bonaparte, and he had explained to me the meaning of the different vestments worn by the priest. Sometimes he had amused himself by putting difficult questions to me, asking me what one should do in certain circumstances or whether such and such sins were mortal or venial or only imperfections. His questions showed me how complex

and mysterious were certain institutions of the Church which I had always regarded as the simplest acts. The duties of the priest towards the Eucharist and towards the secrecy of the confessional seemed so grave to me that I wondered how anybody had ever found in himself the courage to undertake them. (11)

The *auctoritas* is not entirely passive. Father Flynn draws the boy into discussion. He tests him in a kind of catechism, judging the boy's ability to distinguish and categorize: "whether such and such sins were mortal or venial or only imperfections." He wants to see if he can employ this system. Slightly more openly, he asks him "what one should do in certain circumstances," suggesting the beginnings of ethical disputation. This would allow for a more open, critical discussion, but still one guided by an extant, enduring theologic structure. To read with Father Flynn is to take part in a long tradition of repetition that reveals those ancient truths deriving from the godhead. The boy's job—like the priest's—is one of fidelity, his reward that of "knowing," and of being known to know: a member of an elite.

The boy is an apt pupil. Already a "delicate recording device," as Frank Budgen once called Joyce, the boy recalls exact words: "He had often said to me: *I am not long for this world,* and I had thought his words idle. Now I knew they were true." The boy has recalled and reiterated the priest's exact phrase (oft repeated) and registered its triteness. Anyone who employs so timeworn a phrase as "I am not long for this world," is surely merely mindlessly reiterating received language. Here the boy reveals an authorial ability to judge the priest's words, rather than merely to record them: he has noted their shop-soiled weariness.

The boy thinks Flynn cannot really be thinking of what he's saying; he can't mean it. That the priest does indeed mean these words—and that the prophesy they speak is fulfilled—teaches the boy his final lesson as an *auctoritas:* the timeworn words of the past, passed down through the ages, do have power, do signify beyond our intention, which cannot touch their truth. Meaning resides in the words, released by reiteration, ensured of a stable meaning by the Holy Ghost, the guarantor of Tradition: "Now I knew they were true."

And so those other words looming up at the boy: paralysis, gnomon, simony, are also true and powerful, solid as objects, undeniable as death, all the more powerful since the boy does not understand what they mean.

> Now it [the word paralysis] sounded to me like the name of some maleficent and sinful being. It filled me with fear, and yet I longed to be nearer to it and to look upon its deadly work. (7)

The word "paralysis" becomes a marker for the whole of received language, the power of an immense, mysterious, complex Tradition that repeats without alteration, and which cannot be affected by time and interpretation. One cannot, as an *auctoritas,* say anything *about* paralysis that would ever alter its meaning: it exists as a part of God's creation and cannot be twisted from its task of endless iteration of the same.

We can trace in other *Dubliners* tales the same deprecating depiction of auctorial readers. Much of the paralysis of Dublin lies in its readerly piety, passivity, and stasis. Tom Chandler of "A Little Cloud" is clearly a sterile, merely iterative reader, reading located for him as a means of (this time, secular) retreat. He fantasizes about writing (also, as a means of escape) but clearly never will. When his baby's cries interrupt his reading of Byron, his shouted "Stop!" gains richness through its mirroring of the infant's situation. They are equally "without speech" ("in-fant" = without speech), crying out inchoately rather than articulating (giving a shape to) their pain.

As a reader, Mr. Duffey of "A Painful Case" has clearly advanced beyond Tom Chandler. He reads, but also writes. He keeps a diary (appropriating a *Bile Beans* advertisement for its cover) and is translating a Hauptmann play. But these too are purely private and ultimately paralytically reiterative practices. Diaries recount the personal and private; translations repeat their originals. Carefully consigned to the sterile, pale order of Duffey's lifeless room, shut away in his desk, these are his secular devotionals. He has a cogent enough legitimation for avoiding a public authorial role, but one that the *auctoritas* would approve: only the elite can know the truth, and this truth must not be dragged through the streets:

> She [Mrs Sinico] asked him why he did not write out his thoughts. For what, he asked her, with careful scorn. To compete with phrasemongers, incapable of thinking consecutively for sixty seconds? To submit himself to the criticisms of an obtuse middle class which entrusted its morality to policemen and its fine arts to impresarios? (123)

No one in *Dubliners* escapes the auctorial constraint, but in its own punctilious record, *Dubliners* demonstrates how quotation can liberate the subject in language from the enforced reverence of the *auctoritas:* how one may begin to speak for oneself, to become an author through confronting the precise words of the past, of others. The rigorously quotational nature of the tales—actual conversations from Joyce's experience set down without direct commentary—first fulfills the iterative aim of the *auctoritas,* then locates the reader as a maker of meaning. We must, so to speak, add the captions to these photographs. Direct reported discourse is left unprocessed; we are meant to do our own exegesis. By employing quotation, Joyce moves his readers, if not his characters, beyond iteration toward interpretation, beyond the *auctoritas,* toward authorship.

Ultimately, *Dubliners* moves beyond reverence and record to retribution: revenge for having forced one merely to repeat, for having tried to tie language to saying the same thing again and again. Critique supplants commemoration, and Flynn must die that the author may live. Like an extended *Memorabilia, Dubliners* employs the quotational regime against the auctorial dispensation of a presumably stable reiteration. In time, and with different interests, Joyce will move back toward some of the characteristics of the medieval iteration *Dubliners* critiques, allowing language to speak, as the *auctoritas* allowed God to do. Joyce will not always be quotational. But first, he wrote *A Portrait.*

A Portrait: The Quoter's Progress

A Portrait of the Artist as a Young Man depicts the authorial, specifically quotational, triumph we do not see in *Dubliners.* In Stephen's rejection of the Church for the life of an artist, we see the author's victory over the *auctoritas.* Stephen will not repeat—say mass or pray the rosary. He will write; he will be modern; he will turn the tradition—specifically *that* tradition—to his use. By this Joyce admits that reiteration is inescapable, but this iteration, indeed BY this iteration, Stephen will exert his will, define his being, assert himself. He will quote.

And so *A Portrait* begins with a quote, an epigraph from Ovid's *Metamorphoses,* the only of Joyce's major works to employ such an initial device. Linking proleptically with Stephen's concluding invocation to Daedalus ("Old father, old artificer, stand me now and ever in good stead" [257]), the classical epigraph sets the tone of return to the powerful words of the past, but foregrounds their new task as expositor of Joyce's themes, which are not those of Ovid. Broadly one might say that a concern with change joins *The Metamorphoses* and *A Portrait,* but *A Portrait* makes Ovid signify by way of its own interest in progress and emerging identity. These are not Ovid's interests, but Joyce now precedes him.

Having set Ovid, and *A Portrait*'s overcoming of Ovid, at the head of his book, Joyce's narrative proper begins with more quotation:

> Once upon a time and a very good time it was there was a moocow coming down along the road and this moocow that was coming down the road met a nicens little boy named baby tuckoo. . . .
> His father told him that story: his father looked at him through a glass: he had a hairy face.

> He was baby tuckoo. The moocow came down the road where Betty Byrne lived: she sold lemon platt.
> O, the wild rose blossoms
> On the little green place.
> He sang that song. That was his song.
> O, the green wotheth botheth. (7)

Two quotations: one of a story, one of a song. The story's language, like that of *A Portrait* itself, is bent toward its object, the baby Stephen. It is attuned to his language, his way of understanding, and so has, in a way, already been processed and appropriated by him. Stephen then performs a brief exegesis: "He was baby tuckoo. The moocow came down the road where Betty Byrne lived." He links himself with the story, interjecting himself into it, forging a tie between the reiterated narrative and himself. Its source, duly cited ("His father told him that story") and commented upon ("He had a hairy face"), gives way to Stephen's claim of possession of it and its source: *his* father told him that story. Father, story: these are things that belong to him, exist for him.

Then, the song. Unlike the tale, the song is first represented by the text in a source-form that remains proof against Stephen's language, then undergoes commentary by him: "He sang that song. That was his song." The text then reiterates the song in Stephen's lisping voice: "O the green wothe botheth." So the couplet is quoted, precisely, as adults presumably sing it, then Stephen's mutation is registered with equal precision. From the outset of the novel, Stephen processes received language, repeating it, considering its source, calling it his own, altering it in his repetition. The text's stylistic gravitation toward Stephen's mentality performs a similar appropriation: as if Stephen had so fully taken over the language of *A Portrait* that a narrating agent cannot assert an independent voice. If, in *A Portrait,* we see Stephen learn language, we also see him reshape it right from the start.

As the narrative progresses, Stephen's quotational situation moves from a deep susceptibility to others' words to a triumphant, specifically quotational, control over them. At first, we see the powerful effect of words on Stephen: "foetus" sends him spinning into an imagined scenario of enscripture (93), a fragment of Shelley "chills" him, and causes him to "forget his own human and ineffectual grieving" (99), *The Count of Monte Cristo* informs his sense of himself (102). The retreat sermons—those extensive interpolated quotations—move him to terror and submission: "Every word for him! It was true" (128). Prior to Stephen's epiphanic vocational revelation on the beach—itself a rewriting of Jesus' baptismal scene, complete with bird—the words of a valued and reiterated past hold power over Stephen by way of their solidity, their origin in God's creation, and their aesthetic appeal.

Following his rejection of the priestly vocation, Stephen is swiftly shown in a new relation to the canon: that of reader, scholar, reiterator, but also quoter, commentator, critic of the tradition that has formed him. The fathers of the Church become objects of aesthetic rather than ethical appreciation: "he remembered only a proud cadence from Newman" (169). They can serve his purposes, or be set blithely aside:

> His mind, when wearied of its search for the essence of beauty amid the spectral words of Aristotle or Aquinas, turned often for its pleasure to the dainty songs of the Elizabethans. His mind, in the vesture of a doubting monk, stood often in shadow under the windows of that age, to hear the grave and mocking music of the lutenists or the frank laughter of waistcoaters until a laugh too low, a phrase, tarnished by time, of chambering and false honour, stung his monk's pride and drove him on from his lurkingplace. (180)

Quotation, here constituting a kind of time travel, offers Stephen his first chance for flight. As a "doubting monk," he links the givens of his religious formation to the Cartesian project of free thought, but to the demise of the religious. A doubting monk is no monk at all.

Then, even more rigorously, the canon itself is directly attacked. Aquinas and Aristotle are summoned, found lacking, and made to serve Stephen's emergent theory of art. They incite him to speak, but are ultimately in need of Stephen's help: "—Aristotle has not defined pity and terror. I have. I say . . ." (208). Stephen will empty and refill Aristotle's deficient model, as he will for Aquinas, whose "integritas, consonantia, claritas" require translation and explanation by Stephen. Stephen will now tell us what Aquinas means by them; his voice will, in the seeming act of continuing Aquinas's message, supplant it, turning it to his own purpose, which is nothing less than the overturning of the ethical Aquinas with an aesthetic one. Aquinas is made to illuminate Shelley, and vice versa. Stephen lectures Lynch:

> The radiance of which he [Aquinas] speaks is the scholastic *quidditas,* the *whatness* of a thing. This supreme quality is felt by the artist when the esthetic image is first conceived in his imagination. The mind in that mysterious instant Shelley likened beautifully to a fading coal. (217)

"It amuses me," Lynch says, "to hear you quoting him [Aquinas] time after time like a jolly round friar. Are you laughing in your sleeve?" (214). For good measure, more modern sources are found to be equally weak, precisely because they do not accord with Stephen's formulations: "—Lessing, said Stephen, should not have taken a group of statues to write of. The art, being inferior, does not present the forms I spoke of distinguished clearly one from another" (218).

By the end of the book, Stephen quotes himself, a recognition of his entry into the play of quotation, into his full authority. Bad as the villanelle is, it means he has arrived and can iterate with the best of them. "Free. Soulfree and fancyfree. Let the dead bury the dead. Ay. And let the dead marry the dead" (252). Jesus' words quoted then reiterated in new form mark Stephen's continuation with tradition, and his quotational control over it. Liberated from the language of the past, by the language of the past, Stephen is "free."

Ulysses: Citation Beside Itself

Between the satisfying quotational triumph limned in Stephen's *Portrait*, and the citational flotsam trailing in *Finnegans Wake*, lies *Ulysses*, one of the most obsessively scrutinized books ever. It is scrutinized, to a great extent, precisely because of its relation with the great books that precede it; more recently, for its relation with those texts of popular culture that find their way into its pages. Its wholesale rummage through all, and all kinds of, textuality provides rich ground for scholarly action. But for all its voluminousness, *Ulysses* has been thought, by T. S. Eliot most famously, to be controlled and given shape by its Homeric parallel and its other correlative structures. For all its opening the floodgates of allusion, Homer's presence marks that Joyce is in control, an ur-text ordering the mess, one source over and against all the others.

Since Eliot, the project of sorting out *Ulysses*' relation to its encyclopedic sources has continued apace. Don Gifford and Robert Seidman have traced Joyce's "parade of erudition" (1974, preface) with tireless annotations. Weldon Thornton has employed the notion of literary allusion to designate the relation between *Ulysses* and its sources. André Topia has worked out a poststructural approach to its intertextuality in his essay in *The Post-Structuralist Joyce*. As with *Finnegans Wake,* reading *Ulysses* means taking in, processing, interpolating, and sorting out the language of the world, ascribing each word to its proper time, place, and person. To read *Ulysses* is to confront our relation with literature itself. Before it is anything else, it is a reader's read. The Quoter's Progress offered us in *A Portrait* prepares us to read *Ulysses* as quotation, and the Joycean tradition has indeed done so.

Later chapters will undertake to describe how Joyce fell away from this old time religion. But before considering the transgressions of the later work against the propriety of the earlier, the promises of the introduction must be fulfilled. Quotation, if so central to the modern tradition, if so influential to our literacy, must register itself in ways that matter. Part 2, "Inside the Marks: Implications," develops two of the claims implicit in this work so far: that quotation forms the modern subject in and against language, and that quotation supplies modernity with a rhetoric of progress to apply to the past. The next chapter, "Self . . . Style. Joyce . . . Author," returns to *A Portrait* to follow out more specifically how style, that most aestheticized element of the quotational system, serves to ground a modern subjectivity.

Part 2

Inside the Marks: Implications

4
Self . . . Style. Joyce . . . Author

> The coming into being of the notion of "author" constitutes the privileged moment of *individualization* in the history of ideas, knowledge, literature, philosophy, and the sciences.
> Michel Foucault, "What Is an Author?"

Selves speak, and speaking marks the presence of a self.[1] Chilled by the cold sourcelessness of the written, modernity has returned to its rhetoric a speaking self comfortingly present and whole. By way of the inverted comma, language is split and meted out to speakers who are intended as its source, containment, and guarantee. The speaking subject's modern position within language is analogous to that of the referent of the sign: it marks a faith in constant objective reality, a stability and origin that is extra- and prediscursive. By apportioning the linguistic system among speakers, language—not the self—is thought to be split and multiplied.

This modern quotational compensation has intensified a modern premium on style. That is, language specific to a singular self stands as assurance of that self. To read "style" is to see a unique self revealed. Take, as token, Kurt Vonnegut's "How to Write with Style":

> Newspaper reporters and technical writers are trained to reveal almost nothing about themselves in their writings. This makes them freaks in the world of writers, since almost all of the other ink-stained wretches in that world reveal a lot about themselves to readers. We call these revelations, accidental and intentional, elements of style. These revelations tell us as readers what sort of person it is with whom we are spending time. Does the writer sound ignorant or informed, stupid or bright, crooked or honest, humorless or playful—? And on and on. (Vonnegut, in McQuade and Atwan, 197–98)

In what relation does style stand to quotation? Style makes quotation visible, and gives to it an aesthetic appeal that quotation's tedious preoccupation with separation and organization badly needs. Style makes more palatable quotation's work of separation and difference. While the quotational system employs external visual markers (and a legal machinery) by which to designate the source and ownership of language, style is perceived within language itself, identifying in its very fibre a speaking self who uses language in a particular way: Eliot's erudition, Pound's polyglotism, Woolf's evocative metaphoricity. Style and quotation are part of the same system, complementary means of affixing a signature. Quotations are signed after the fact, as it were, from the "outside," while style means seeing the person inherently present in language, signed all over the "inside," deliciously unique, voluble, endearing, revealing. For modernity, all styles are signature styles.[2] Only in a modern era of quotation could style have achieved such prominence.

Modernity departs from classicism not in the recognition of distinct styles; Quintilian identified the grand style, the middle style, and the simple. But these are clearly thought of as means any speaker may learn to use, not in order to define his personality or personhood, not to "express him*self*," but rather, after Aristotle's *Rhetoric,* to attune language to its object, to match the treatment to the topic. Style, for Aristotle, is a matter of fidelity to the referent (the "spoken of"): the speaker is merely a conduit, a means. If a particular speaker's *ethos* is enhanced by the skillful employment of an appropriate style, we have to remember that *ethos* is nothing like "personality," but rather signifies one's moral standing in a community. *Ethos* is one's credibility, not one's "self." Aristotelian mimesis sees the ideal speaker as an invisible one, and in this we recognise Aristotle's rather uncomfortable status as a rhetorician.[3]

The etymological trace of "style" as it is woven into modernity bears many of the same characteristics as "quotation." Both are caught up in the apparatus of the written. By way of an associative transformation, both come to indicate the language of a distinct personality. The earliest definitions of "style" denote a writing implement, the "stilus" of antiquity, and by a metonymical association, a manner of composition. By the mid-sixteenth century, "style" comes to mean the giving of a name, as well as indicating a form of written work. The later sixteenth and seventeenth centuries adopt the coincidence of writing and naming by using the term to indicate a written manner particular to a single person: a signature style. By the early nineteenth century, "style" is not only a characteristic[4] attribute of one's language, but has been generalized to indicate how one appears to others, especially in the choices one makes concerning dress. If clothes make the man, style—in clothes, in words—ensures his discrete status within a shared language that threatens such autonomy, such "self-naming." By way of style, the self signs itself into signification, as all selves must.

The nineteenth century's ultimate jointure of soul and style was perhaps most influentially articulated by Walter Pater, whose 1889 essay "Style" joins the literary genres of poetry and prose in their common attribute of style. "Literary art," writes Pater, "is the representation of . . . fact as connected with soul, of a specific personality, in its preferences, its volition and power" (Pater, 1599). While Pater still ultimately considers subject matter the most important element of a work, Oscar Wilde extends Pater's emphasis on style, saying in a review of "Style," "Truth is entirely and absolutely a matter of style" (305), and "there is no art where there is no style, and no style where there is no unity, and unity is of the individual" (356). With both the beautiful and now the true riding on the authentic individual, the stakes of style within modernity are very high indeed. As a visual marker of difference in language, style comes to signal authentic difference between modern subjects. The figure of the author serves as the prime example of the essentially unique individual: the living, speaking self who marks his uniqueness, vitality, and selfhood with every word. Style serves to convince us all that we are, indeed, individuals: that which cannot be separated.

A Portrait: A Speaking Likeness

Joyce did not "invent" the figure of the author ex nihilo, any more than the romantic poets did. It was established enough at his arrival for a very young Joyce to step into a certain version of it, and profit from it: Joyce was a professional writer long before he had actually published anything of note.[5] But if he did not originate the figure, he was a powerful continuer of it, and Joyce is thought of today as something like the archetypal modern author. I would claim that this is largely attributable to the fact that James Joyce's works depict, precisely, the author, continuing and developing the figure throughout his canon. Established as an object of study during the era of New Criticism, when the academy was committed to the excision of the author *of* the text, Joyce satisfyingly offered an author *in* the text (see chapter 7).

First and foremost, it is as the author of *A Portrait of the Artist as a Young Man* (1916) that Joyce defined himself both as an author and as the author and his masterful status within and against language. As the author of this articulation, Joyce himself is scripted as the perfect fulfillment of his own figure. Collections of biographical anecdotes about Joyce are titled *Portraits of the Artist*.[6] Chester Anderson's brief biography uses *A Portrait* as a primary source on the growth of the author Joyce.[7] The man Joyce hovers over his work, a final referent, an ultimate proof of the truth of the book: after all, the evolution of the author we see depicted is depicted by the fully evolved author.

It is in this sense of the utter believability of *A Portrait*, its utter acceptance as *reality* that the power of Joyce's version of the author can be gauged. For if the first reception of *A Portrait* was anything, it was a reception of recognition: this was really it. John Harris's review claims that "*A Portrait of the Artist as a Young Man* is not only an original book; it strikes us as fundamentally true."[8] *Everyman* intoned, "The description of life in a Jesuit school, and later in a Dublin college, strikes one as being absolutely true to life." "The interest of the book," said H. G. Wells in the *Nation*, "depends entirely upon its quintessential and unfailing reality. One believes in Stephen Dedalus as one believes in few characters in fiction." If Stephen could be welcomed as a *true* depiction, then this particular form of the artist/author was not exactly new: rather, his figure and status were *recognized* and recognizable to the reading public. With *A Portrait,* Joyce gets taken up as the very voice of the author: it is his (Joyce's, "the author's") defining document. If, to modernity, Stephen Dedalus/James Joyce somehow *is* the author, what kind of author is he? What is his relation to language, and where do style and the self come in?

First of all, in a recirculation we find familiar, the question of Stephen and language *is* (famously) the matter of the book. This is its innovative modernist gimmick: the book's mastery of language and of style grows along with its object, a double *bildungsroman*, an Aristotelian throwback. When very young, Stephen is facinated with the mysteries of naming:

> It was very big to think about everything and everywhere. Only God could do that. He tried to think what a big thought that must be but he could only think of God. God was God's name just as his name was Stephen. *Dieu* was the French for God and that was God's name too; and when anyone prayed to God and said *dieu* then God knew at once that it was a French person that was praying. But though there were different names for God in all the different languages in the world and God understood what all the people who prayed said in their different languages still God remained always the same God and God's real name was God. (*Portrait*, 16)

Coming to terms with linguistics in a distinctly Saussurean way, Stephen first recognizes the identificatory function of language (God knows who is French), then its puzzling arbitrariness ("there were different names for God in all the different languages"), but ultimately reasserts its ability to signify a stable referent across languages: "God remained always the same God." Finally, Stephen comes to confirm "God's real name," that is, the name he himself calls Him. Language, then, has power over those who speak it, in that it names and defines who they are. But it also lends to its users power to know the presumably true nature of things beyond language's mediation: God's real name.[9]

But there are other powers language can impart, as is made clear in the "do you kiss your mother?" episode of chapter one. Here, Stephen learns language can establish a power relation not in what it says, but in its very activity. Language does more than *mean*, it also *acts*. Joyce adds J. L. Austin to Ferdinand de Saussure:

Wells came over to Stephen and said:
—Tell us, Dedalus, do you kiss your mother before you go to bed?
Stephen answered:
—I do.
Wells turned to the other fellows and said:
—O, I say, here's a fellow says he kisses his mother every night before he goes to bed.
The other fellows stopped their game and turned around, laughing. Stephen blushed under their eyes and said:
—I do not.
Wells said:
—O, I say, here's a fellow says he doesn't kiss his mother before he goes to bed.
They all laughed again.... What was the right answer to the question? (*Portrait*, 14)

There is no answer, for while this is a question with content, the content is not at issue: both answers are equally risible because the question is not a communication of meaning, not a *real* question, but a thing done to Stephen, an attack. (Visitors to Ireland have noticed how often the Irish will answer a question with another question, perhaps a residue of the habit of deflecting interrogation.) That language has this power to do something to one, to force bodily reaction (a blush) and a fundamental reversal of claim (Stephen changes his answer), is an important lesson for a writer to learn, even if he is, in this case, the done to rather than the doer. Stephen will in time become the inquisitor, making it his goal to enact on the body of Ireland just such an attack. He will learn to make language both signify and act *for him.*

Man's precedence and control over language is reasserted, even at its earliest stages of learning as Stephen, the poet *manqué,* becomes quiveringly aware of the sensual world of color, texture, temperature, and (especially) sound. For Stephen, the seemingly empirical "rightness" of language, its onomatopoetic tie with the sensory world it represents, is learned very early:

> Suck was a queer word. . . . But the sound was ugly. Once he had washed his hands on the lavatory of the Wicklow Hotel and his father pulled the stopper up by the chain after and the dirty water went down through the hole in the basin. And when it had all gone down slowly the hole in the basin had made a sound like that: suck. Only louder. (*Portrait,* 11)

The action of sucking says its name, a perfect onomatopoeic match, a true representation. But if language is not always quite so right as this, if it sometimes seems to be puzzling and nonsensical (after all, the above reflection is triggered by a prep-school usage, "suck = apple polisher," a meaning not as clearly referential as the correspondence of "suck" and the sound of the drain), that is merely a matter for effort. Thought and work can subdue language's ways. One learns that "belt" means both a strip of leather or cloth and a blow, and these have a certain association. One can learn that red maroon velvet on the back of a brush can somehow be connected with Michael Davitt, can "stand for" him, and that green can do the same for Charles Stuart Parnell. Metaphor, rather than shaking faith in the stability of language, becomes one of its most beautiful and satisfying elements:

> Eileen has long thin cool white hands too because she was a girl. They were like ivory; only soft. That was the meaning of *Tower of Ivory* but protestants could not understand it and made fun of it. One day he had stood beside her looking into the hotel grounds. . . . She had put her hand into his pocket where his hand was and he had felt how cool and thin and soft her hand was. She had said that pockets were funny things to have: and then all of a sudden she had broken away and had run laughing down the sloping curve of the path. Her fair hair had streamed out behind her like gold in the sun. *Tower of Ivory. House of Gold.* By thinking of things you could understand them. (*Portrait,* 42–43)

It is in this taking on of the burden of demonstrating man's precedence over language that Stephen's much-discussed Christlike qualities stand most clear.[10]

Stephen's use of language, though like other people's, is unlike, too. For, from the outset, Stephen demonstrates a grasp of linguistic play that is understood to be somewhat special. His earliest consciousness is already a consciousness of words: he quotes (indirectly) his father's telling of the story of Baby Tuckoo. And while still small enough to hide beneath tables, Stephen already responds to Ireland's threats with poetry.

> He hid under the table. His mother said:
> —O, Stephen will apologise.
> Dante said:
> —O, if not, the eagles will come and pull out his eyes.
> Pull out his eyes,
> Apologise,
> Apologise,
> Pull out his eyes. (*Portrait*, 8)

Stephen manifests the figure of the author in precisely the romantic vein: sensitive, attuned to the world, naturally and from the first manipulating language. Later, he will demonstrate those elements of isolation, truth-telling, exile, passion, and martyrdom that will fill in the fuller picture: the artist in but not of the world, part of a brotherhood that spans time.

> Welcome, O life! I go to encounter for the millionth time the reality of experience and to forge in the smithy of my soul the uncreated conscience of my race. . . . Old father, old artificer, stand me now and ever in good stead. (*Portrait*, 25)

By the end of the book the narrating agent, which has established itself as problematically Stephenic, is abandoned, and *A Portrait* joins itself fully with its object. It is given over to Stephen's diary: direct quotation, in that the voice of the novel has turned its right to speak over to Stephen. So here is Stephen's very voice, written down—a speaking likeness—and we can begin to read not *A Portrait,* but a book within a book that is *Stephen writing*. A diary is an appropriately private, appropriately protestant form, a form of the self, and Stephen's is clearly a kind of workbook, documenting a young man's private struggle toward the mature artist's public contribution. As before, in his struggles over the villanelle that would not come right, here in the diary we see the craftsman searching for his topic and style:

30 March: This evening Cranly was in the porch of the library, proposing a problem to Dixon and her brother. A mother let her child fall into the Nile. Still harping on the mother. A crocodile seized the child. Mother asked it back. Crocodile said all right if she told him what he was going to do with the child, eat it or not eat it. This mentality, Lepidus would say, is indeed bred out of your mud by the operation of your sun. And mine? Is it not too? Then into Nilemud with it!
1 April: Disapprove of this last phrase. (*Portrait,* 250)

Recording narrative with an eye toward form, rejecting a tarnished mentality, the young Stephen hones his craft, for "he would create proudly out of the freedom and power of his soul as the great artificer whose name he bore, a living thing, new and soaring and beautiful, impalpable, imperishable" (*Portrait,* 170).

It is in this authorial freedom, in this sense that even the material of his production—language—cannot conform his activity, that *A Portrait* grasps and articulates the kernel of the author's contribution to the modern self. That he fulfills a mythic model already prepared (that this freedom already has a name he "bears"), that he considers and admits the derivitive nature of his view, an admission itself learned from Lepidus ("mentality . . . bred out of your mud"), suggests the modern ambivalence of this self in language.

Language, nation, and religion: these are the "nets" Stephen would fly by (*Portrait,* 203); they are the interwoven nets of a textuality Stephen seeks to reject. But in flying by them, is Stephen understood to escape them, to elude their power? Or will he *fly* by them, by means of their textual material? This ambivalence is precisely the point of quotational anxiety on which modernity balances.

If *A Portrait*'s matter is the acquisition and use of language, it is also its manner. Stephen and style emerge together, in a teleological trajectory that leads, in a familiar *ricorso,* back to the author of *A Portrait*: the mature author James Joyce. If the narrative voice is not quite Stephen's, it closely parallels his acquisition and mastery of language. This may be the crux of the book's believability: that style, in true Aristotelian fashion, conforms to its object, performing an impersonation that reproduces on the level of "author" something more like the discourse of the character than we are used to. This is one of Joyce's most effective tricks of verisimilitude: in a story about growth, about maturation, the prose and its object interact and grow together.

Hugh Kenner calls this stylistic interaction "The Uncle Charles Principle," named as such after the particular citation where Kenner first divines it in *A Portrait:* in a description of Stephen's Uncle Charles "repairing" to the outhouse to smoke. "Repairs" is precisely the word Uncle Charles would have employed to describe his action. Kenner reminds us that this swerving of style towards its object is not only characteristic of *A Portrait*, but typifies the Joyce canon in general:

> This is a small instance of a general truth about Joyce's method, that his fictions tend not to have a detached narrator, though they seem to have. His words are in such delicate equilibrium, like the components of a sensitive piece of apparatus, that they detect the gravitational field of the nearest person. (Kenner, *Joyce's Voices,* 16)
>
> The Uncle Charles Principle entails writing about someone much as that someone would choose to be written about. (Kenner, 21)

For Kenner, however, the author's status is never questioned by this stylistic swerving: there is always Joyce, pulling the strings. He insists there is no serious blurring, and that, in *Ulysses* for example, Bloom and his narrator are kept distinct even under the assaults of that most troubling—to the notion of distinct subjectivity—of narrative techniques: the interior monologue. Ultimately, in order to relieve the worry such stylistic infidelity engenders, Kenner posits *two* narrators for *Ulysses:* a "good" one, who tries to move the story along, and a "wild" one, who flaunts his stylistic disruptions. Here again we see the contestatory two, battling for dominance.

With the Uncle Charles Principle, Kenner has put his finger not merely on an interesting attribute of Joyce's stylistic variance, but on precisely the point of uncertainty to which Joyce's texts bring us. Kenner recognizes style is meant to define the authorial self, and that Joyce's prose can flicker between different styles, different speaking selves. This stylistic mobility begins to disturb a sense of a controlling authorial presence, and we begin to feel the need for the "detached" voice that would mediate responsibly between character and reader: that would use style in the way modernity needs it to be used.

Joyce's stylistic swerving becomes even more disturbing as it moves, in *Ulysses,* into the interior monologue. There, the interior monologue takes citational ownership to an extreme and enacts its undoing. It moves the reader not only into a world wholly constructed of a character's consciousness, but into a book that, in large part, is pure quotation: a presumably verbatim record of Stephen's and Bloom's minds. But this quotational context, far from laying out the distinction of the subject in language (as modernity intends it to do), only foregrounds its destruction. This is not just a matter of asking "who wrote the headlines in 'Aeolus'?," that first instance of an anonymous textual voice intruding into *Ulysses* (though the narratological indeterminacy of that gesture demonstrates how various are the ways by which Joyce undermines the narrating subject). In less overt ways, even at that point when we ought most to believe in the equation of quoted language and the modern self, do we sense an instability that is irredeemable.

So, even as the interior monologue would seem to be the ultimate fulfillment of the quotational system of separation, definition, exactitude—the very essence of the human self captured in language—it begins to destabilize that economy of fulfillment. We begin to suspect the unitary "mono" of a monologue Jacques Derrida calls "ingenuous."[11] If the interior monologue seems to be "all character," to give us precisely the voice of the object, it never quite entirely loses its sense of the presence of another, or other, voices. We are moving in and out, from inner voice to outer narration, so fluidly as to preclude complete attribution. Hear Mr. Leopold Bloom at breakfast.

> Cup of tea now. He sat down, cut and buttered a slice of the loaf. He shore away the burnt flesh and flung it to the cat. Then he put a forkful into his mouth, chewing with discernment the toothsome, pliant meat. Done to a turn. A mouthful of tea. Then he cut away dies of bread, sopped one in the gravy and put it in his mouth. (*Ulysses*, 55)

"Cup of tea now." That sounds like Leopold Bloom's talk. Then we are "outside," in the voice of the narrator for a simple description of his morning meal, as simple as Bloom might himself have written it. Would Bloom have used "shore"? And what about "chewing with discernment the toothsome, pliant meat"? That sounds like advertising copy, but when we remember that Bloom is a canvasser of ads, it seems as if we might attribute it to him. "Done to a turn." Whose? "A mouthful of tea." Does one really talk to oneself in quite this way when one is eating? Isn't this telegraphic status report necessarily the exigency of the narrator? Where then, is the narrator? And, if Bloom thinks in clichés and advertising copy, precisely who is he? These are the questions the indeterminacy of the text leads us to ask. It is our modernity that finds them important.

The proper attribution of language—a necessity increasingly felt in Joyce's work—is further complicated by Joyce's refusal to use quotation marks, neither the English inverted comma nor the French *guillemet*.[12] Joyce insisted on the dash to indicate direct reported discourse, with the result that, while one can identify with accuracy when a character begins to talk, it is impossible to identify precisely when he or she leaves off, and the narrator takes over again.

Anonymous voices, refusal to punctuate "properly," the Uncle Charles Principle, and the interior monologue—what Joyce does and what Joyce fails to do—these mean that to read Joyce is to find first seemingly confirmed then utterly eroded a quotationally assured place within—or rather, above—language. These points of disturbance are, however, recuperated into the authorial tradition as more proof of its accuracy: they are all attributes precisely of Joyce's *style:* ironic, parodic, comedic, incongruous, difficult. These are points of technique that *prove* rather than undermine his place in language.

Sensing the identificatory flickering Joyce's prose can cause, founders of the Joyce Industry anxious to establish his authorial rights and his unique style sought to maintain subjectivity's borders, both through referring any points of uncertainty back to Joyce and in explicitly theorizing the moment of writing as a contestatory, citational one. Richard Ellmann's *The Consciousness of Joyce* undertakes to establish a citational distinctness we can trust even at that point where it might be most under seige: in the moment of writing. In *The Consciousness* we see played out Joyce's creative battle with his sources, and we see him emerge the victor: the book will show how "Joyce assimilated . . . works into his own without giving up his individuality, how in fact they gave him added power" (Ellmann, *Consciousness,* 9). Ellmann carefully defines the creative consciousness where this conflict is staged:

> "Consciousness" denotes the movement of the mind both in recognizing its own shape and in maintaining that shape in the face of attack or change. Joyce's consciousness declared itself in certain initial choices. (Ellmann, *Consciousness,* 1)

Even for Ellmann Joyce's consciousness is already double, but no more plural than that. In proper Cartesian fashion, it is both a stable entity of a certain shape and a consciousness that perceives and defends that shape from outside influence: a consciousness and a self-consciousness: a mind and a mind that minds that mind. Choice, intention, control, in short, the ability to establish borders, are seated in this second order or metaself. This is the Joyce who chooses, assimilates, and controls source material. This is the Joyce who *quotes*. Ellmann intends to demonstrate "How he distorted or consolidated his materials, in the service of bringing them into a new verbal existence" (9). Bordered citation rules, even and especially at the moment of creative enscripture. These two techniques, then, for answering queries about the author: invoke his intentional stylistics and affirm his citational control. Style and citation work together to affirm his stability, power, and prestige.

Can these means of damage control: the telling of writing as quotational mastery, the invocation of intentional comedics (irony, parody, incongruity) entirely assuage a suspicion of authorial control the Joycean text itself engenders? We are caught in a contradiction, and the tension of this incongruity surpasses that means of explanation. To answer a question about the author with an appeal to the author is only to reiterate the question, not to move toward an answer. Joyce is all style, but while that "style" ought to name him, to mark his fashion of being, to define his borders, it becomes the precise ground of his problematic. Joyce exhausts style, and after him, the equation self = style = author is no longer reliable.

In the fatigue following the completion of *Ulysses,* Joyce wrote Harriet Weaver, "I suppose the law should take its course with me because it must now seem to you a waste of rope to accomplish the dissolution of a person who has now dissolved visibly and possesses scarcely as much 'pendability' as an uninhabited dressing gown" (quoted in Ellmann, *Joyce,* 512). At the end of his "odyssey of style" (Lawrence), Joyce is dissolved in that sea he has traversed. No need to hang him; being "undependable," he will not hang.

The Wizard Endures

Little of what I have written above about Joyce's undermining of the modern subject is new. Contemporary Joyce criticism has in many and various ways dismissed or problematized Joyce the master writer. In fact, to reintroduce the figure of Joyce the autonomous author, as Margot Norris does in *Penelope's Web* (1992), counts, Norris admits, as "theoretically retrograde" (Norris, 8). But if such a move is theoretically retrograde, it is hardly institutionally shocking. Polysemy, bricolage, heteroglossia, intertextuality: these are still generally understood as Joyce's, institutionally bound within the territory of his works, and organized within the discipline of Joyce studies as a theoretically informed field. Nowhere are the implications of Joyce's authority more likely to be contested than at one of the many conferences or symposia dedicated to him precisely as a great modernist (perhaps *the* great modernist) author. The 1995–96 volume of *James Joyce Quarterly* features Joyce's image on three of its four covers. To liberate Joyceans from Joyce would mean a radical rewriting of language itself, a liberation that would drain Joyce studies of the juicy humanist appeal that sustains it as a popular, as well as an academic, interest. When it attempts such a liberation, criticism runs against the brick wall of Joyce's personal prestige. Lesley McDowell and Catherine Driscoll, for instance, in the preface to their forthcoming *Joyce's Daughters,* claim that "To say daughters of Joyce, or *Joyce's Daughters* . . . is not necessarily to posit any woman or woman character as subsidiary to or less authentic than Joyce." But in this they are fighting a losing battle. The power of the possessive is not to be denied. In "Joyce's daughters" Joyce is doubly primary: as Joyce, the author, and as Joyce, the author of these girls' beings.

In short, contemporary theoretical scepticism about the figure of the author may urge its readers to pay no attention to the man behind the curtain, but the Wizard is clearly visible. Joyce's text violates the figure of the self, even as it delineates it, and this teasing antinomy can be expected to endure within Joyce criticism, not the least because criticism itself retains most adamantly the quotational regime. When we cite, we cite Joyce. Himself.

5

Modern Citation, Modern Historiography

> Continuous history is the indispensible correlative of the founding function of the subject: the guarantee that everything that has eluded him may be restored to him; the certainty that time will disperse nothing without restoring it in a reconstituted unity; the promise that one day the subject—in the form of historical consciousness—will once again be able to appropriate, to bring back under his sway, all those things that are kept at a distance by difference, and find in them what might be called his abode.
>
> Michel Foucault, introduction to *The Archaeology of Knowledge*

History is a problem for modernity. As the very ground on which modernity stands, the past is crucial to the modern as a sign of what it has exceeded. That was then. This is now. Where we have arrived. We've come a long way. Modernity needs the past, but as a corpse, a dead and stable point on a map, by which modernity may chart its progress. Modernity needs the past, and a gap between itself and the past, a distance by which to measure its identity as the modern. "Modernism is," writes Perry Meisel, "in all its historical manifestations, the recurrent desire to find origins or ground despite the impossibility of ever doing so for sure" (Meisel, 9). Surpassing the past, the modern must still find it readable, must still bear a close enough relationship to it to trace a reliable difference.

Modernity needs the past, but must also and instantly reject it, must claim so radical a break with it that its necessary connectedness becomes a strain. It is this, if anything, that marks modernity: the claim to a new age. The term itself comes from fifth-century Latin, meaning "in our time," a word by which the Christian era was bordered from the pagan. *Our* time, set in careful opposition to *their* time: the time of classicism, the ancient world, however periodized. That other but not Other time must remain both readable and proximate (in order to gauge this difference that marks modernity) and at the same time uncanny and strange. This modern difference can mean a sense of progress or a sense of loss. "Modernism strongly implies," write Richard Ellmann and Charles Feidelson, "some sort of historical discontinuity, either a liberation from inherited patterns, or, at another extreme, deprivation and disinheritance" (Ellmann, *Tradition*, vi).

Currently, we have the same difficulty with claims to postmodernity, that newest of new ages, variously imagined as an epistemic, aesthetic, or political break with modernity.[1] But if we—newly identified as "postmoderns"—can know we have exceeded the modern, and chart precisely in what ways we have done so, have we indeed moved so far from it? If we can understand and explain the old *episteme* (and if we still feel the need to "understand" and "explain"), have we entirely broken with it? Hal Foster describes the problem. He asks:

> how can we exceed the modern? How can we break with a program that makes a value of crisis (modernism), or progress beyond the era of Progress (modernity), or transgress the ideology of the transgressive (avant-gardism)? (Foster, ix)

Or, we might add, evade modernity's preoccupation with identity by assuming another, "postmodern" one? To supercede an era is precisely the modern move, yet another claim to a historical and epistemic break with the past. The tension between historical continuity and historical change must first be recognized as a concern arising within the modern itself.

In order to determine the difference that marks modernity's separation from the past, the past must remain readable. When we, as moderns adopting the task of the historian, look at the traces left by the past (and all that remain to the modern historical eye are the past's representational traces), our modernity depends on a certain continuity with them. We must be able to make the words and images of the past yield not just difference (which might not be at all readable) but a certain kind of difference. We must be able to read in such a way as to demonstrate modernity's transcendence over a past we can, for all our temporal separation from it, comprehend in its actuality.

Now, the problem of whether and in what way the historian can get at the *actual* events of the past preoccupies the modern historian, and frequently serves as the initial gesture in reflections on the nature of history.[2] History is both event and account of event. The urge for an empirical historical accuracy rises in the eighteenth century with the rise of other scientific expectations, such that, writes Hayden White,

> Nineteenth-century European culture displayed everywhere a rage for a realistic apprehension of the world. . . . in spite of their generally scientistic orientation, the "realistic" aspirations of nineteenth-century thinkers and artists were informed by an awareness that any effort to understand the historical world offered special problems, difficulties not presented in the human effort to comprehend the world of merely physical process. (White, 45)

These special problems had to do with the fact that historical event is proper to man, and so was thought ineligible to be objectively observed by him. Yet this necessity for the "real" persists, both as an epistemological necessity and as an ethical one. For seeing the world and its history as it really is makes possible that other great tenet of modernity: progress. White explains how

> historical thinkers during the greater part of the nineteenth century were as interested as their eighteenth-century counterparts had been in providing the bases for belief in the possibility of "progress" on the one hand and some kind of justification for historical "optimism" on the other. For most of them, the concept of "progress" and the feeling of "optimism" were compatible with the "realistic" world view to which they hoped to contribute through their historical writings. (White, 47)

White's own historical project schematizes various nineteenth-century approaches to the telling of this truth of history. But the presumably second-order fact of history's writtenness (White's primary concern) remains, for the historian of the first order, a serious problem well into the twentieth century.[3] This historian's task, undertaken in the glare of expectation of objective truth, is to amass and describe the documents of the past, deriving from them a "true" world view that can serve as the grounding for modern self-knowledge and historical progress. Attention to language has ever troubled the wish for direct access to truth,[4] and under the onus of this scientistic expectation, *telling* the truth becomes the more problematic.

The Past Speaks for Itself

This question of the reliable readability of the past, then, locates a crucial question for modern self-identity.[5] It also brings us back to the topic of citation, for where is the past read in the texts of the present? By what rhetorical system is this relationship between the present (modern) reader and the textuality of the past negotiated? Precisely in the rhetoric of quotation, where intertextuality is contained in such a way as to order and control modernity's confrontation with the past.

In what way does bordered quotation provide for just this modernity? First, and perhaps most crucially, quotation allows the past *to speak for itself*. In the same way that the cited passage affirms that here is another real voice, another real individual, it also affirms that here is another authentic time. To quote functions rhetorically to make the past live again, to allow it to speak in its own words. In its work as particularizer and identifier, style functions for the temporal gap precisely as it did for the individual. In foregrounding "historical" differences of dialect, diction, or grammar, the past is marked as authentically different, authentically surpassed, and authentically represented (since we do not represent it; it represents itself). *Quotare*, to separate and count, allows a separation between and an accounting for a reliable, demonstrable historic difference.

This return of voices of the authentic past, while a functioning tenet of modern history's project in general, reaches a newly central articulation in social history. Take, for example, Carlo Ginzburg's 1966 work on witches in the sixteenth and seventeenth centuries. Delving back into interrogation records of the late Inquisition in northern Italy, Ginzburg's *The Night Battles: Witchcraft and Agrarian Cults in the Sixteenth and Seventeenth Centuries* will return to us "the voices of these [interrogated] peasants," for

> The principal characteristic of this documentation is its immediacy. Except for the fact that the notaries of the Holy Office translated the testimony from Friulian [the local peasant dialect] into Italian, it is fair to say that the voices of these peasants reach us directly, without barriers, not by way, as usually happens, of fragmentary and indirect testimony, filtered through a different and inevitably distorting mentality. (Ginzburg, xvii)[6]

In addition to reconstructing within his own rhetorical interests the "conversations" between suspect and inquisitor, Ginzburg appends in full one of the interrogation transcripts to the volume (a kind of ultimate quotation), so that we may see the actual source material "illustrated," though "obvious errors have been corrected" (Ginzburg, 147). That these are the records of the Inquisitor might be one obvious point of suspicion of them, but it is a point that E. J. Hobsbaum, in his introduction to the work, attempts to blunt.[7] Authentic quotation subtends undisturbed the claim for Ginzburg's historical validity. By quoting (listening) to the voices of the past, one can gain access to a history of authentic fullness: the real thing.

Moreover, one can apprehend its specific difference from us. When we read one of the voices of the peasants, carefully translated for us first from Friulian into Italian, then from Italian into English, we can, by virtue of the linguistic and temporal work of translation, see in that far distant time practices that are bizarre, but readable as such; strange, but not uncanny. Ginzburg cites an Inquisition witness describing one fertility cult, the *benandanti*:

> Sometimes they go out to one country region and sometimes to another, perhaps to Gradisca or even as far away as Verona, and they appear together jousting and playing games; and . . . the men and women who are the evil-doers carry and use the sorghum stalks which grow in the fields, and the men and women who are benandanti use fennel stalks; . . . and when the warlocks and witches set out it is to do evil, and they must be pursued by the benandanti to thwart them, and also to stop them from entering houses, because if they do not find clear water in the pails they go into the cellars and spoil the wine with certain things, throwing filth in the bungholes. (Paolo Gasparutto, cited in Ginzburg, 3)

Ginzburg can set this narrative in a historical context that explicates it. His book's argument is that a benign fertility cult of *benandanti*, who ritualistically fought evil spirits so that harvests might be plentiful, was cast by the late Inquisition into the Church's version of standard heretical witchcraft. Such matrices of superstitious beliefs, as well as the religious institution that Ginzburg shows suppressed them, are equally demonstrative of the distance we have traveled from such systems. The voice of the modern historian returns to the documents of the past, and in the stroke of his explication both revives the true past and demonstrates our modern difference.

But quotation does more than set up a reading of history that is authentic and carefully different. It also provides for the sense of *progress* modernity requires. Quoted fragments (even those of one's contemporaries) are cited as superseded, for if one does not *further* the words of those others, of the past, why write? Each writer or speaker is clearly located in a now, and cited texts are situated as a past backlog of language the citing speaker has come *after*. It is true, that, as we cite, we often attribute to the ideas and words of the past (often under the mark of the speaking persons of the past) the courtesy of the present tense: "Kant claims . . . , Clausewitz suggests . . . , Marx interrogates. . . ." But this etiquette serves rather to reinforce a modern conquest of the past—that the ideas of the past are now made *present* in two ways: here, and now—than to undermine chronology. When we read "Kant claims . . ." no one imagines that the writing philosopher or historian is under the impression that Kant is still alive. Through the use of the present tense, the quoter's relationship with the quoted is understood to take place in the now of the citing author. But Kant's quote is thought as the voice of Kant himself and carries with it Kant's era, complete.

Every writer exists in a present, is writing for himself, *now*. This is one of the many strange things about reading quite ancient texts: that their writers presume the immediacy of a present when they are quite clearly past. And it is even odder that this does not really strike us as odd. But while every speaker and writer exists, as he or she writes, in the present, every citation always already exists in a past. It is this function of modern citation that provides us with a simple, linear sense of textual—and historical—sequence. A quotation is both an authentic living voice speaking its own words, and the reliable mark of the true deadness of that past.

Best of all, the citing text enacts this surpassing of the past before our very eyes. First allowing the past to speak authentically and in its own words, the bordering text carries on the work of paraphrase, interpretation, and critique, recontextualizing the past according to more current concerns. In the very time of the reading itself, the past is both resurrected and reinterred. As a part of modern citation's intrinsic function as sequencer and hierarchizer of voices, texts that quote assure us of two things: that the past is different and that this difference is a controllable one that can only return to us our modern difference. Modernity is different from the past, but can recount and account for all the ways in which it is different, that is, better (or, for the antimodern modern, worse). Modernity *masters* the past, quotes (cuts off, separates, and counts) it *as the past*, and demonstrates its modern recontextualization.

The formal system of quotation arranges this controlled difference of modernity. For the always-present-tense writer to enclose a fragment of the past, to use it, to read it is to signify implicitly a history that has altered in content, but not in form. Or, to say it another way, for quotation's history, events have occurred, but none that would threaten our readerly access to the past. Times change, but language never does. Quotation insists on the readability of the past, and implicitly, on the sameness of language, wherein history becomes, as E. H. Carr puts it, "an unending dialogue between the present and the past" (Carr 35).

In the metaphor of conversation, Carr raises the question of the language in which the present and the past might converse. If both the present and the past will have their say, in what language will they speak: that of the present, or that of the past? And, if the present can understand and speak the words of the past (or, if the past speaks the language of the present), precisely where are we to draw the line between them? Where is the radical epistemic break on which modernity rests? For modernity, the historicity of language itself must be ignored or explained away. Carr, for instance, does both:

> The historian is of his own age, and is bound to it by the condition of human existence. The very words which he uses—words like democracy, empire, war, revolution—have current connotation by which he cannot divorce them. Ancient historians have taken to using words like *polis* and *plebs* in the original, just in order to show that they have not fallen into this trap. This does not help them. They, too, live in the present, and cannot cheat themselves into the past by using unfamiliar or obsolete words, any more than they would become better Greek or Roman historians if they delivered their lectures in a *chlamys* or a *toga*. (Carr, 28)

But while the historian belongs to the present on the level of language, Carr assures us that history "is not a matter of words alone" (28). First taking seriously the possibly profound gap between the languages of the past and the present, Carr reduces them to particular terms in which he can localize and limit the problem of language as a *system* in which all elements work together. His specific appeal to clothing suggests Carr's attitude toward the function of language as a superficial covering for concepts that are transhistorical. Whether you call it a *toga* or a robe, somehow not much is lost in the translation between languages and between eras. Why mince words? There are bigger fish to fry, for "the function of the historian," Carr adds, "is neither to love the past nor to emancipate himself from the past, but to master and understand it as the key to the understanding of the present" (29).

Reading historians, then, must objectively comprehend the documents of the past (apprehend "reality"), and recontextualize them in the concerns of the present (make "progress"). They must quote. They are engaged in a process of mastery by which the past is both readable (exists in the same representational field) and useable (can be attuned to modernity's needs). But for all its attempt to embrace a *real* history, quotation institutes a history that is radically ahistorical, a history of continuity, a history of tradition and similarity that would erase any real doubt as to the availability of the past. Modern history is made reliable in the sense that it can be counted on, not in the sense that it is "the real thing." Quotation, as the rhetorical container for both this "reliable" (rather than real) apprehension and this masterful recontextualization, institutes a particular modern history's possibility.

Saying the Same Thing Twice

Modern history rests on the belief that while times change, language never does. We can always read the texts of the past authentically and derive both historial truth and our modern difference, because we dwell in the same horizon of signification as the past. We can read the past and get it right, because language repeats itself exactly. One can *say the same thing twice*. Before we move on to discuss the ways in which moder*nism* in general and Joyce in particular took up modernity's quotational project, it might be useful here to describe the ways in which citation may not guarantee this readable historical difference, but may rather present modernity with a past that is unaccountable (unquotable).

In "Signature Event Context" Jacques Derrida takes on philosophy's notion of writing, a version that bears a clear resemblance to that of history above. The version he will describe and question is, in fact, "*the* system of interpretation, or in any case of all hermeneutical interpretation" (Derrida, 175). Ultimately, Derrida is interested in teasing out of the assumption of precise repetition of language an irreducible plurality that undoes the notion of repetition itself.

Following the term "communication" out to its various seemingly stable meanings, Derrida points out the way in which the concept of "communication" splits and multiplies, can suggest this import or that, and that what is generally seen to act as a check on this kind of "polysemy" is *context*: that the word is used in this setting (here, academic prose) rather than that one (say, an architect's plans). "But," asks Derrida,

> are the conditions [*les requisits*] of a context ever absolutely determinable? . . . Is there a rigorous and scientific concept of *context*? Or does the notion of context not conceal, behind a certain confusion, philosophical presuppositions of a very determinate nature? . . . a context is never absolutely determinable . . . its determination can never be entirely certain or saturated. (Derrida, 174)

Very soon, a problem within the accepted notion of "context" arises, and arises, not surprisingly, specifically at the place where *writing* enters the field of communication. For at the same time that the addressee is presumed, in modern interpretive practice, to be capable of "absolutely determining" between contexts, Derrida points out the way in which the space of communication is already imagined as a *homogenous* one, *without* contextual variety. "To say that writing *extends* the field and the powers of locutory or gestural communication presupposes, does it not, a sort of *homogenous* space of communication?" (Derrida, 175).

In search of more specific characteristics of this continuous space of communication, Derrida reads Condillac's "Essay on the Origin of Human Knowledge" as "an explicit reflection on the origin and function of the written text," which he takes as token of the interpretive tradition at large. With Condillac, we are

> within a philosopical discourse that, in this case and throughout philosophy, presupposes the simplicity of the origin, the continuity of all derivation, of all production, of all analysis, and the homogeneity of all dimensions [*ordres*]. . . . hence writing [itself] will never have the slightest effect on either the structure or the contents of the meaning (the ideas) that it is supposed to transmit. . . . The same content, formerly communicated by gestures and sounds, will henceforth be transmitted by writing. (Derrida, 176)

Here we are back with E. H. Carr, carefully reading the thoughts of prior subjects, thoughts which have been in no way affected by their linguistic containers. Language and history do not affect signification and we can be certain that when we read, we are enacting a reliable replay of original intention. Writing does not get in the way of language repeating itself precisely, a function it *must* perform in order to "communicate" across the gap between sender and receiver, between the past and the present. Here Derrida begins his torsion of the argument:

> A writing that is not structurally readable—iterable—beyond the death of the addressee would not be writing. . . . there is no such thing as a code—organon of iterability—which could be structurally secret. The possibility of repeating and thus of identifying the marks is implicit in every code, making it into a network that is communicable, transmittable, decipherable, iterable for a third, and hence for every possible user in general. To be what it is, all writing must, therefore, be capable of functioning in the radical absence of every empirically determined receiver in general. (Derrida, 180)

Two characteristics, then, of what Derrida characterizes as "the classical concept of writing." First, that writing must be repeatable beyond the writer's or receiver's absence or presence. That it must have a life of its own. Second (and this is really just part of the first), writing must be able to break with the conditions of its enscripture, it must "break with its context" (Derrida, 182). Having dutifully followed Condillac out to this point, it is clear that we have actually departed in a very radical way from the "classical" version of communication Derrida claimed he set out to trace.[8] The history of interpretation requires that language be iterable (across time, among subjects) but this very iterability, for Derrida, must abort any attempt at claiming a contextual homogeneity, a continuous fabric of language. That trope that is meant to ensure the readability of the past, is, after Derrida, precisely that figure that most problematizes it. Signs repeat, but wholly apart from an originary restraint or contextual grounding. That is, *without carrying a stable or readable history with them:*

> Every sign, linguistic or non-linguistic, spoken or written (in the current sense of this opposition), in a small or large unit, can be *cited,* put between quotation marks; in so doing it can break with every given context, engendering an infinity of new contexts in a manner which is absolutely illimitable. This does not imply that the mark is valid outside of a context, but on the contrary that there are only contexts without any center or absolute anchoring [*ancrage*]. . . . What would a mark be that could not be cited? Or one whose origins would not get lost along the way? (Derrida, 185–86)

At the very point of modern historical continuity, then, lies a break. Language, which will and must allow for iterability, repeatability, readability, for saying the same thing twice, does not allow that second saying to tie itself to the first. Everything is both fundamentally citational—already said—and unimaginably new. The point is that there is no way for the singular modern subject—so often counted on to sort out contradictions of this sort—to arbitrate this difference, to trace both the continuity and schism with the past. We are neither free from the past, nor fettered to it. Derrida's notion of citation disallows this bordering off of past from present, for repetition is everywhere and nowhere, a condition of our existence and not an object by which to interrogate and docket that condition as "new" or "old." We've inverted Montaigne's problem. While he worried how to say something new, now the anxiety is whether or not one can ever repeat.

Joyce and Modernist Citation

Modernism, inheritor of modernity's quotational relationship with the past, participates in it in ways that ultimately make it a problem, and a problem very much of the sort Derrida has outlined above. (Derrida's history is a stringently modernist one.) Modernity, from the seventeenth-century quoting to preserve and control the past *as the past,* begins its slide into modernism's late-nineteenth- and early-twentieth-century quotational revision just at this point of confidence: that the past could be brought, reliably, into the present for review. Ezra Pound's goal for modernism, that it "make it new," suggests both the necessary presence of the texts of the past in those of the present, and the priority of the present. To "make it new," we assume "it"—the material of art—is old, a given. Fundamentally preoccupied with the museum of the past, modernism's "disappointed professors"[9] cited heavily. But it is generally understood that they did so as a means of effacing the past: of demonstrating its ineluctable collapse into the fluctuating consciousness of the present.[10] Those who consider this dominance of the present a central tenet of *post*modernity's relationship with the past will find it instead firmly entrenched in modernism's quite early understanding of itself, an understanding based firmly on standard modern practice. Donald Marshall describes modernist literature's strategies for this kind of escape, among which is numbered citation:

> Originality, novelty, the absolutely outrageous are efforts to break the chains of history, but they show that history had first to be conceived as chains. Myth, symbol, and the varied appropriations from religion are not only attempts to capture religion's cultural role, but a project to discover for literature resources proper to it yet able to rival the success of its chief antagonist, science, in escaping history. Even allusion, borrowing, and parody are devices to evade historicality by establishing a decontextualized immediacy. (Marshall, xviii)

Many of the memorable historical schematizations modernism embraced emphasize the inseparability of the past from the present, where the past is collapsed into or contained within the present. T. S. Eliot's "Tradition and the Individual Talent," for instance, lays out a continuous, progressive notion of literature in which "No poet, no artist of any arts, has his complete meaning alone. His significance, his appreciation, is the appreciation of his relation to the dead poets and artists." Similarly, the Poundian concept of "paideuma," an anthropoligical term passed to Pound by Leo Frobenius, suggests all the inherited, shared, and continued systems joining people in a particular culture, "from their 'ideas' down to the things they know in their bones," says Hugh Kenner (*The Pound Era,* 507). Wyndham Lewis's notion of vortex, in that it derives from a Poundian figure, not surprisingly suggests a similar jointure of past and present, being "race consciousness . . . all the artist does not invent but must know" (*The Pound Era,* 238). History, culture, inherited patterns swirl about the head of the artist, and are sucked down into his unifying apprehension. Likewise, Yeats's 1925 *A Vision* details yet another modernist sense of historical continuity, the theosophical notion of reincarnation, a literal rebirth of the past in a repetitive historical cycle. Human character, political structures, and aesthetic development are, in the words of "The Second Coming," "turning and turning in the widening gyre." Not merely repetitive, for each of these models, the eternal return is a return of the same, and time, bereft of teleology, becomes reduced to a recurrent round of iteration.

James Joyce, too, for all of his early preoccupation with shedding or transforming his own and Ireland's past,[11] came to envision history as cyclic repetition. For Joyce, the dead return to haunt the living, a young man named Dedalus (again) becomes an artist, and a Homeric hero finds a modern avatar. This cyclical vision is most explicitly articulated in *Finnegans Wake*, where Joyce takes up Giambattista Vico's *Scienza Nuova* (1744) and its three stages of history, each equipped with appropriate aesthetic and political correlates: Theocracy, Aristocracy, Democracy, and a *ricorso*, a coming round again. Richard Ellmann explains how:

> In all his books up to *Finnegans Wake* Joyce sought to reveal the coincidence of the present with the past. Only in *Finnegans Wake* was he to carry his conviction to its furthest reaches, by implying that there is no present and no past, that there are no dates, that time—and language which is time's expression—is a series of coincidences which are general all over humanity. Words move into words, people into people, incidents into incidents like the ambiguities of a pun, or a dream. We walk through darkness on familiar roads. (Ellmann, *Joyce*, 551)

History, that project of reclaiming and controlling the past, within modernism acquires inverted commas; "history" is everywhere and nowhere; it is the "nightmare" from which modernism tries to awake, and the material of waking consciousness; "these heavy sands are language tide and wind have silted here," intones Joyce (*Ulysses* [hereafter cited as *U*], 3.88–89). While modernity quotes to demonstrate an ordered progression from the past to the present, modernist quotation is thought to display the result of such a too-successful temporal conquest: an indifferent phenomenolized hegemony of the "now." Hugh Kenner describes how:

> Joyce's prime assumption routinely baffles newcomers: that there is, cognitively speaking, no "past." There is only what we can experience, as it streams through "the eye of a noodle" (*FW* 143.09). True, we can write what we call "history," an effort to account for features of what we experience.... But such "histories" are stories—fictions— and themselves exist in the present, alongside what they propose to

explain.... "What might have been and what has been," mused T. S. Eliot in a similar vein in "Burnt Norton, "Point to one end, which is always present." (Kenner, "Joycean," 853)

History, in this view, has been neatly handled, rendered moot by the phenomenonalization of textuality, as it flows "through the eye of a noodle." And, indeed, the reception of *FW* has been one that precisely foregrounds its domination of time, beginning with Marcel Brion's 1929 essay in *Our Exagmination,* where he claims for *Work in Progress* a "ubiquity," that makes for a new "universe, the Joycean world, which obeys its own laws and appears to be liberated from the customary physical restraints" (*Our Exag,* 33). Thinking *FW* as a dream has opened it most persuasively to those critical practices that incidentally exclude historical analyses, as Margot Norris's structuralist analysis and Kimberly Devlin's psychoanalytic work, in their reading of the text's repetition as myth or neurosis, demonstrate.[12] Neither James Fairhall nor Robert Spoo considers *FW* in his treatment of Joyce and history, Spoo suggesting that the exposition of the Viconian correlates seems to have counted as covering, even exhausting, the topic (Spoo, 10).

It begins to look as if history has been written out of *FW,* as it has indeed been written out of modernism in general, relegated to the indifferent and repetitive telling and retelling of one narrative after another, more grist for the modernist mill, more fodder to feed a perception of the present. But if, in essence, Joyce and modernism delve into the past only to smelt it into the present, what has happened to history? In turning *FW* into a document that demonstrates modernity's power over the past—a reading fundamentally formed by modern quotation's shaping rhetoric—we denude it not only of its ability to do more than tell us about the current telling of history, but to actually constitute a historical event in and of itself.

If modernism assumes it can say the same thing twice, and in the second saying colonize the first into the time of the now—precisely what *FW* is thought to do—Derrida's suggestion that a second saying may not tie itself to the first challenges us to look again at *Finnegans Wake,* considering carefully whether its "comings round" can be joined in the interest of Viconian order, thematic consistency, mythic recurrence, or psychoanalytic insight. To cut, for instance, each occurrence of the litter free from the previous one, is both to identify its relation—or this cannot be recognized as iteration—and to (re)place it in an irreducibly new context from which its signification begins again, uncannily familiar and utterly new. In short, can we reduce repetition in *FW* to quotation's law? What would it mean to refuse to do so?

Modern Citation, Modern Historiography 77

Richard Ellmann's use of the term "universal history" to describe FW captures its problematic place in modern citation's project. Appropriately enough, "universal history" itself derives from a particularly odd incidence of attributional confusion. Ellmann describes Joyce's plan for the book:

> The impression Joyce gave Harriet Weaver was that he was using the dream form, as once he had used the internal monologue, "as a convenient device," because of its "shiftings and changes and chances ... allowing the freest scope to introduce any material he wished—and suited to a night-piece." This was the 'universal history' of which Joyce has spoken to Miss Weaver; it would mix history and fable in a comic leveling. (Ellmann, *Joyce*, 544)

But "universal history" was not what Harriet Weaver told Ellmann Joyce said, and the quotes around it are more than a little disingenuous. In the passage where Ellmann describes this event—Joyce speaking to Weaver of his plans—he quotes Weaver quoting Joyce as saying, "I think I will write a history of the world" (1956 interview with Harriet Weaver, quoted in Ellmann, 537). Within the quotational indeterminacy of who said exactly what, Ellmann coins a phrase he finds useful, by his own lights, to describe Joyce's intent, and attributes it to him via Weaver.

Ellmann's phrase is as unstable as its origin. "Universal history" is self-contradictory, for universality is precisely not historical, but eternal. Universality effaces the historical, rubbing away difference to produce an ahistorical and presumably everlasting truth. Ellmann continues this notion in claiming that Joyce had "conquered time" (Ellmann, *Joyce*, 597). To call *Finnegans Wake* "universal history" identifies it precisely as a modern document, one that undertakes the project of mastering, subordinating, and ultimately swallowing the past and the past's difference. To the extent that the *Wake* is thought to perform this mastery, it is a definitively modern text, its relationship with the past controlled and stablized. It becomes yet another metanarrative toward which postmodernity looks with "incredulity."[13]

But is it? "Universal history," this modern/ist name, is not after all Joyce's phrase, but Ellmann's. Harriet Weaver, from the extraquotational messiness of the oral, trying to recall the gist or spirit of what Joyce said, tells us he intended to write "a history of the world," and in this phrase a fundamental difference is suggested. To write *a* history is not to universalize, but to recount in particular, and on a local level. It is to write of the world, not of the universe, of the proximate, not the grandiose. To think of *Finnegans Wake* as a pre- or postmodern text means giving up the ordering separations and universalizing generalities modernity's textual rules establish. History is clearly all over the *Wake*. But must it be made "universal," thereby effacing very real energy and multiplicity? Rather than insisting on a unifying, universalizing voice or principle, couldn't the *Wake* give voice to but precisely *not* encompass or contextualize the past? Might it actually break with both modern and modernist assumptions about time, history, and the past?

Reading *Finnegans Wake,* we sense history's presence, but can neither date its origin nor trace its precise effects, for it is without modernity's signposts: quotation marks. The *Wake,* in its disregard for citational bordering, recalls a prequotational economy of texts Joyce himself pointed toward when he likened *Work in Progress* to the work of Laurence Sterne. As such, Joyce's last work can be seen to fit firmly into textual tradition, but a tradition that precedes the printing press's alterations in our view. In the end, *Finnegans Wake* can sustain neither modernity's need to objectively reclaim the past, nor modernism's need to efface it. However, its very inefficiency can bring us closer to acknowledging what our modern(ist) necessity is. Postmodernity, as we read it in Joyce's last work, does not mean doing away with history, as has been claimed.[14] That is a modernist narrative. Rather, postmodernity and the *Wake* call us to a new sense of the presence of the past, a relationship to it that is a claim for neither authentic reclamation nor dominating effacement. The *Wake* may confront us with a past that is, in a single word, unaccountable.

So far, we have considered modern quotation's evolution, its collaboration with style and the author, and its hold on our reading of the texts of the past. The next and final section traces further Joycean offenses to the rule of the quote. The first argues for a resistant, eroticized Irish orality articulated through the women of *Ulysses*. The second takes interest not in Joyce reading, but in readers of Joyce: as Derrida has called them, "that mighty family," the Joyceans, and how their quotational obedience wavers in the face of Joyce's seductive way with words.

Part 3

Beyond Quotation: Resistances

6

Moomb

—I am not thinking of the offense to my mother.
—Of what then? Buck Mulligan asked.
—Of the offense to me, Stephen answered.
Buck Mulligan swung round on his heel.
—O, an impossible person! he exclaimed.
James Joyce, *Ulysses,* 1.219–21

Stephen is not thinking of the offense to his mother. But he is thinking, this morning in June, of little but his mother. Her undead presence hangs between Buck and Stephen. She and her final illness are signified, through Swinburne and A.E., by the wide bowl of the green sea. Stephen's capacious memory recalls "her *secrets:* old featherfans, tasselled dance cards, powdered with musk, a gaud of amber beads in her locked drawer" (*U,* 1.255–56), laying these relics of youth and beauty against his dream image of "her wasted body within its loose graveclothes giving off an odour of wax and rosewood, her breath, bent over him with mute *secret* words, a faint odour of wetted ashes" (*U,* 1.270–73, emphases mine). Impossible to elude, May Dedalus becomes to Stephen a "Ghoul! Chewer of corpses! No, mother! Let me be and let me live" (*U,* 1.278–79).

Stephen's emphasis on the secrecy of May's things makes poignant the fact that he knows just what is in that locked drawer. Her secrets have been taken from her, part of a totalized maternal sacrifice. She can hold nothing back from her voracious family, which then, in classic projection, casts her as the inescapable, grasping presence, a "Ghoul! Chewer of corpses!"[1] Her words, mute and secret like her things, are equally offered up for family use. But they pass, like the food, clothing, comfort, and sympathy she provides, through the being of her son, translated into his representation of them.

In association with his mother, Stephen remembers physical things: her mementos, her body, her breath. Ever alive to words, he does not remember hers, but rather recalls her body, and its products. Bile, not language, emerges from her mouth. Her words are refracted through Stephen's perception, undergoing there a seachange: the words of a dead woman are modified in the guts of the living. She is made "mute." Not just dead, she is, as Buck Mulligan calls her, "beastly" dead, an animal who never had language. Calling her "beastly" (like an animal unable to speak) is not, for Stephen, an offense to his mother, but to himself as a wielder of memorable words.[2]

Here in *Ulysses,* May is mute, her language reported indirectly, with one exception. Stephen recalls some of her words, when she is speaking of words: those of Yeats's "Who Goes With Fergus?." "For those words, Stephen: love's bitter mystery" (*U,* 1.252–53). When May Dedalus is quoted by her son, it is only to hear her pointing up and repeating the words of another: she does not turn them to any purpose of her own, but will plead only that they be repeated. (Stephen complies. "Who Goes With Fergus?" follows him throughout his day.) He quotes her quoting, a conduit of language between Yeats and Stephen, not an initiator of her own words. Joyce drew a good deal of memorable language from his father ("Shite and onions!"), but is there no word from the mother? While Stephen (and Joyce) recognize the power of a father's words, to quote the mother is somehow out of the picture.

May Dedalus's excision from quotability and quoting happens in the revising and aestheticizing of the *Stephen Hero* manuscript into *A Portrait of the Artist as a Young Man.* In *Hero,* far from a silent and aliterate presence, May is singled out by Stephen as a commentator on his work, and as a reader of Ibsen's. The *Stephen Hero* manuscript shows her far more conversant as a reader and thinker than her husband. Stephen, having sought her out to read her the essay he will deliver to the UCD Literary and Historical Society, discovers his mother's readerly past.

> I'm surprised to hear you ask about Ibsen. I didn't imagine you took the least interest in these matters.
>
> Mrs. Daedalus pushed her iron smoothly over a white petticoat in time to the current of her memory.
>
> Well, of course, I don't speak about it but I'm not so indifferent . . . Before I married your father I used to read a great deal. I used to take an interest in all kinds of new plays.
>
> But since you married neither of you so much as bought a single book!

Well, you see, Stephen, your father is not like you: he takes no interest in that sort of thing ... When he was young he told me he used to spend all his time out after the hounds or rowing on the Lee. He went in for athletics.

I suspect what he went in for, said Stephen irreverently. I know he doesn't care a jack straw about what I think or what I write. (*Hero*, 85)

Peering inside this secret drawer, Stephen has found not fans and dance cards, the detritus of courtship, but the memory of a relationship with words, and with reading. May's premarital reading, about which she "of course" does not speak, has been effaced by her marriage, printing replaced by petticoats. The fact of her reading emerges and is opposed to Simon Daedalus's sportsmanly anti-intellectualism. Stephen's hearing the news of his mother's early intellectual interests leads him not to a reflection about her past literary life—we might have expected him to want to know just what his mother did read—but rather to a denunciation of the father. And May's readerliness is immediately placed under submission to another man: her son.

I would like to read some great writer, to see what ideal of life he has—amn't I right in saying "ideal"?

Yes, but ...

Because sometimes—not that I grumble at the lot Almighty God has given me and I have more or less a happy life with your father—but sometimes I feel that I want to leave this actual life and enter another—for a time.

But that is wrong: that is the great mistake everyone makes. Art is not an escape from life!

No? (*Hero*, 85–86)

Stephen goes on to set her right, offering a somewhat muddled realist manifesto. Later, after May has read several of Ibsen's works, the insufficiency not only of her escapist literary theory, but of her self-awareness is revealed. Reading *A Doll's House,* she finds Nora Helmer, whose marital confinement might have been expected to strike home to her, "a charming character" (86). Does May's approval of Nora slyly include approval of her desertion of her family? We'll never know: Joyce seems ultimately more interested in locating her in an escapist bourgeoise insensitivity, Barthes's readerly consumer. Her escapist approach means she cannot recognise her own condition when it is baldly presented to her. So much for mirrors held up to nature.

Stephen's self-absorption returns the book to his preoccupations, and May's premarital intellectual interests are forgotten by the manuscript of *Stephen Hero*, then excised altogether as *Hero* becomes *A Portrait*. By *Ulysses*, May has become the ghostly and mute emanation discussed above, horrific not for what she has to say, but for what she is: an undead presence.

It is one of the many delights and complexities of *Ulysses*—a book that proceeds largely by way of the language in men's heads—that it concludes, or at least ends, with Molly's soliloquy: finally a presumably full and unmediated reporting of what passes in a woman's mind. Until then, women's words are indeed "secret" and "mute," modified and represented through various narrative screens—Gerty MacDowell's language, for instance, is refracted through the lens of the chapter's pulp fiction conceit—or documented as events in Bloom's day and quickly subject to his interpretation: Milly and Martha Clifford's letters, the other end of his conversations with women. The exception is the dream episode of "Circe," where the narrative conceit of a stage play provides us with directly reported language attributed to women, but, as Bella becomes Bello, we can never be quite certain of a stable gender behind it. The quotable woman seems, like Stephen but in a far more radical sense, to be an "impossible person." But there are two issues to deal with here: whether and in what way a woman can quote others (May intoning Yeats) and whether a woman can herself be quoted (Stephen recalling May's precise words).

Can the feminine be quoted when the act of quoting, of engaging in the egoistic struggle with prior language is scripted as masculine? As a trope of ownership, authorship, and singular origin, as a system of dominance and control, the quoting author is surely masculine. One who quotes is always already masculinized by the very act of cutting off and controlling another voice. Unless we imagine a prequotational gesture of simple repetition—much as May Dedalus is shown making—the quoting woman is an "impossible person," instantaneously invalidated by the gendered dynamics of the rhetorical game.

Woman cannot herself quote, but can she then, be quoted? One would imagine that she is the one who precisely *can* be quoted, taken and made to speak at the bidding of man. Or, to put it another way, that all quoted material is in some way always already feminized (certainly emasculated: it is precisely "cut off") by the act of being quoted. But here, too, we encounter a problem, for in the general economy of quotation, those who are quoted are themselves quoters, members of the long line of readers in the tradition. Authors take it in turn playing master and slave, quoter and quoted, but the quoted, too, derives from authorial origin. Both sides of the subjectival split instituted by quotation are thought to be stable and ultimately masculine, in order for the oedipal conflict to play itself out. Women's voices are turned to masculinized authors the moment they set pen to paper. It is just this problem of recuperation that works such as Jacques Derrida's *Spurs* or Luce Irigaray's *This Sex Which Is Not One* try to counter and evade, thinking woman not as woman author, as *Madwoman in the Attic* authors Sandra Gilbert and Susan Gubar, (and, in another way, early Helene Cixous) would do, but rather as an incommensurate, unchartable force or voice in language, speaking not as a man, but from within a feminine enigma and elusiveness: May's secrecy and muteness.

Given this exclusion of woman from the modern quotational structure, the question of where and in what way women may write, exchange texts, or refer to previous words, again rises. If the quoting agent, of whatever biologic sex, is understood as a masculine figure of mastery and control, how can a woman's voice be heard? As I have tried to show above, the economy of modern quotation is by no means an efficient one, requiring a policing structure of immense proportions to enforce its dicta. One option, embraced by some Marxist or avant-garde presses, is to forgo copyright, a kind of dropping out or away from the external commodification of texts. "Copyleft" embraces the free exchange of ideas while attempting to avoid their appropriation to the capitalist system. However, since the books are sold for money, and their authors (even if anonymous or plural) cited according to the rules, such works are ultimately returned to the dominant citational dynamic. Refusal of copyright, either in print or electronic media, has yet really to threaten quotational economy.

More individualized strategies of resistance are already in play. Kathy Acker, for instance, scripts a prose that foregrounds the question of literary ownership by brazen theft. In the recontextualization or revision of the canonical, her work transforms its sources, but not as the romantic author transforms his source into something "his own," but precisely to foreground the problematics of citation: this is clearly cribbed. An almost mechanistic transformation occurs when Dickens is appropriated into her violent and visceral work *Great Expectations,* but Dickens is neither mastered nor Ackerified. He resides uncomfortably inside the work, influencing it and influenced by it. Acker's text does not fall into any of the categories quotation sets up. Echo, allusion, quotation, paraphrase: none name this act. The defining intent to deceive is lacking, for she precisely does not attempt such a deception, advertising rather than effacing her appropriation. Yet she imports significant chunks of others' works, titles, plots, characters, such that Kevin Dettmar has suggested the term "piracy" rather than plagiarism as illustrative of her extraquotational moves.[3] Before it signified plagiarism, "plagiary" meant kidnapping.

While presenting a problem to citational definition, Acker's piracy, along with other appropriative "postmodern" techniques of collage, pastiche, parody, replication and reappropriation of found objects (such as that found in the work of Andy Warhol, Tom Stoppard, Jorge Luis Borges, or Barbara Kruger) have themselves been commodified, identified with particular authors and movements, precisely fulfilling the modernist avant-garde agenda of originality quotation subtends. Warhol is thought to *use* the found and appropriated image of the Campbell's soup can, and it becomes his, a signature piece, a hallmark. Appropriation, like most avant-garde strategies meant to escape the modern and the modernist, ends up reinscribing it in its very originary form. And this is perhaps modernity's most totalizing moment: that resistance and intervention are reclaimed by the modern metanarrative of progress and mastery as just the next new thing.

In order to articulate a broader base of quotational resistance and to fit the feminine into it, it is time to recall the founding cultural phenomenon on which quotation rests, that is, literacy and the revision of consciousness that came in the wake of writing. We may find an alternative in orality, the rhetoric in place prior to our shift to the written. Orality (or more precisely for already literate cultures, residual orality) can work against, elude, or evade the rigidities of the written, and can do so as a particularly feminine strategy. Before tracing this resistant orality in Joyce's *Ulysses,* where it is specifically associated with the feminine, how has the split between orality and literacy been thought?

Orality vs. Literacy

First we must remind ourselves of a problem. Any thinking we do about orality will necessarily be from the perspective of modern literates (you are, after all, reading this). Consequently, what orality is (for those few cultures that maintain it) or may have been (for most of us, who have lost it) becomes a project of reclamation problematic in the same way as other contemporary reclamation projects: the voices of women "reclaimed" by masculine interpretive means, the voices of the poor "reclaimed" by the middle class, the voices of the uneducated "reclaimed" by the educated, the non-Western "reclaimed" by the Western. Describing an oral *episteme* from a position after its effacement—an effacement which radically changed our thinking—puts us at risk of skewing our notion of the oral into a literate (or simplistically antiliterate) one.

Walter Ong's important *Orality and Literacy: The Technologizing of the Word* (1982) notes the way the literate west has turned oral cultures (definitively non-Western) into its Other, characterizing them as *illiterate* rather than *nonliterate,* ignorant, superstitious, irrational, illogical, and incapable of thought. The problem is vividly depicted in Lucien Levy-Bruhl's 1928 *Primitive Mentality* that, while decrying ethnocentric assessments made by Christian missionaries and early anthropologists as shortsighted and wrong, again and again falls into the same frustrated negativism, demonstrating the difficulty of finding a new way of approaching the nonliterate even if armed with an awareness of the difficulties. Levy-Bruhl's lexicon of thought, suggested by his book's title, is already charged and limited.

Ong, however, feels he has got it right, and if one senses a strongly romanticized nostalgia for a lost oral community in his assessment of nonliterate cultures, his work is all the same impressively detailed and well thought out. Please note, that far from claiming that Ong is right about orality—about which I am not, for the reasons described above, qualified to judge—I want only to point out the consonance of his notion with Joyce's work. Ong's first point is that orality is not the *il* or *un* of the literate, but is really quite different from it. He builds on the field work of Milman and Adam Parry, Eric Havelock, and others to define several characteristics of oral thought, characteristics that emerge from the material conditions of having no means of record but the human memory. "In a primarily oral culture," Ong writes, "to solve effectively the problem of retaining and retrieving carefully articulated thought, you have to do your thinking in mnemonic patterns, shaped for ready oral recurrence" (Ong, 34). The resulting thought is:

1. *Repetitive and formulaic.* Because memory is aided by repetition, oral language circles back on itself as a way of reminding speakers of the story so far. Set phrases, epitaphs and truisms (as in Homer, an oral work) recur as a means of keeping touch with the known. Orality is thus circular rather than progressive, more concerned to retain and maintain than to supersede or progress beyond (Ong, 41).

2. *Additive, not subordinating.* Ideas tend to stand side by side in oral language, in a chain rather than a pyramid or hierarchy. The paratactical "and . . . and . . . and . . ." structure of many Biblical passages is thought to be a remnant of this thought pattern, one that is systematically rooted out by literate translators (Ong, 37). Main ideas and subordinate details are inventions of a literate thought that can backscan in order to keep both

systems (the "facts" and the relationship between them) straight. Thus, oral thought tends to be characterized as simplistic, rather than structured in a wholly different way, with a different purpose.

3. *Aggregative, not analytic.* This is another way of saying the above. Language bears the burden of remembering the past, of conserving the wisdom and knowledge of the culture. As such, it tends to organize ideas in clusters that resist breaking apart. One does not speak of a soldier without using the epithet "the brave soldier," or of an oak without attaching its primary quality, "the sturdy oak." Thus, orality is ideologically conservative as a function of its mnemonic conservation. The analytic turn of breaking such idea-packages apart, of distrusting the values they attach to words (are all soldiers brave?) is a particularly literate development.

4. *Situational, not abstract.* Oral thought is tied to the immediate lifeworld. It is pragmatic. When nonliterate subjects are shown a picture of a hammer, a saw, a log, and a hatchet, and are asked which does not belong, their answers vary according to their judgments about the best way to deal with a log. But none reject the log as "not a tool," as children in literate cultures routinely do. The category "tool" is an abstraction existing in literate thought, not in the immediate press of lived existence. Oral subjects think rather in terms of actual situations. In most oral cultures there is no word for "intelligence." Respect is paid some skilled member of a community because of a particular ability, not because of some invisible essential quality. One is not "smart"; one is a good navigator, and the matter is left at that (Ong, 51, passim).

These specific characteristics exist for Ong in a more general understanding of human life as communal, interactive, and nonobjectified. Language derives from a speaking human, who is a living presence, even if much of what she or he says is understood as, and valued for, its status as inherited. Source, then, is doubly present, in the voices of ancestors and in the current speaker. Language is never distinct from human interaction, is never objectified as a thing. To the oral mind, there is no such thing as grammar.

Similarly, speakers do not objectify themselves either as autonomous or as thingly. That unselfconsciousness that literates like Rousseau and Montaigne find so endearing in "savages" is part of orality's resistance to abstraction. One does not step back to view oneself as an object of study, or a thing outside of oneself. Identity is fixed by external rather than internal influences. Modern self-analysis—and paradoxically enough the field of linguistic anthropology itself—is a highly literate practice and value. Meanwhile, the oral subject says, "What can I say about my own heart? How can I talk about my character? Ask others; they can tell you about me. I myself can't say anything" (Ong, 55).

Finally, while orality's speech is laden with the presence of the past, it is in itself "evanescent" (Ong, 32). It occurs in time as writing occurs in space. Speech is invisible and fleeting, an event, not an object, existing only as it passes. Because language always derives from a living being, and itself moves, it seems to live, while writing, solid, static, and impersonal, is associated with death and the dead.

It is clear from this brief overview that Ong's version of orality participates in the metaphysics of presence Jacques Derrida critiques in *Of Grammatology*. Literacy's relatively recent "restructuring of consciousness" (*Homo sapiens* has been literate for only about 9 percent of its history) involves the breakdown of what Ong thinks of, in a clearly nostalgic way, as the "natural" (Ong, 82). Orality, whatever it may actually be, for literate moderns is intrinsically associated with a close, warm, human community integrated with itself and the natural world.

Literacy, on the other hand, plays the dark other to this cozy scene. With it come the evils Plato warned of: the weakening of the memory, the dehumanizing of man. But most of all, with the internalization of the new technology of writing into the modern psyche, a wholesale objectification of the world begins, the transmutation of lived experience into a fragmented panorama of dead things, seen through the filter of immobile, impersonal, unresponsive script. Discourse, and thus human interaction, through the intervention of writing, becomes in this dynamic autonomous, free of context (or any particular context) that would locate it in a here and now, with these particular people as audience. Its source is absent and problematic, its relation to the past worrisome, its reader silent and passive. Ultimately, subjectivity under literacy objectifies itself as a self in a way orality does not, and the solitude and isolation of reading and writing that replaces the warm presence of orality puts presence itself at issue: the author's or the reader's own.

This fairly standard depiction of the oral/literate split clearly already traces a gender difference that is equally standard: women, and especially Joyce's women, like "primitives," are easily associated with the oral: communal, pragmatic, sitational, resistant to the abstract, the logical, or the self-conscious. They are simple, conservative, unreflective. Their thinking is local, and "evanescent," in the sense that it does not last, any more than May Joyce's words have persisted. Men (in general but not generally in Joyce) are awarded the literate side: impersonal, logical, abstract thinkers, sceptical and philosophical, more interested in generating lasting new knowledge (making progress) than in retelling the tales of the past. If women repeat old wives' tales, men write complex, revolutionary novels like *Ulysses*.

Since there are varying levels of orality and literacy within different cultures and indeed within individual speakers, orality and literacy, rather like the masculine and feminine hormones, are in tension, each with their own claims. Joyce, growing up in the strongly orally residual culture of Ireland (Ong, 86), worked through the competing worldviews of orality and literacy in his writing. To remember him composing, as he usually did,[4] at the kitchen table or in a cafe, voices buffeting him, is to capture something of the situation every culture faces: a tension between the world of the voice and that of the letter. This tension is both depicted in and constitutive of *Ulysses*. Beyond this general claim for Joyce's work, which I will only have opportunity to sketch rather than fully develop, I want to argue more specifically for an association of this notion of the oral with women in *Ulysses*, a particularly Joycean orality that plays Ong's standard description in a warmly eroticized key.

Joyce and Oral Sexuality

I suppose you could say that *Ulysses* is both speech and writing. It is obviously a written work; Joyce was a writer. But a writer of a particular sort, with a particular project. The interior monologue, depicting as it seems to do the ground zero of language—human consciousness—would seem to capture inner voices. Readers of *Ulysses* tend to think of its textuality as somehow authentically *spoken*. Hugh Kenner maintains that these are *Joyce's Voices*. *Ulysses* is read aloud, marathon style, or in dramatic performance, and this seems somehow right. Anyone who has heard Fionulla Flanagan read the "Penelope" episode has probably sensed that those words have come home to their true medium in the spoken word. After a highly literate excursus: stylistically experimental, demanding, complex, objectively represented, requiring analysis, the work returns to its preliterate origins: a verbatim record of a woman on the edge of consciousness, a lyrical recording of language flowing through her head. "Penelope" is Molly Bloom's monologue, a spoken performance. It is the last word before the music of *Finnegans Wake*.

In every episode of *Ulysses* the hallmarks of orality are intertwined with those of the written.[5] We move from the highly literate Stephen Dedalus at one extreme, to women, who—especially when they write—are furthest from the literate world and closest to an orality that defines their femininity. Women in Joyce don't read much and seem to have a peculiar relationship with what they do read. Not quite illiterate, at least in the strict sense, they are all the same figures that resist the literate. By contrast, Stephen, the work's most highly literate figure, thinks precisely along this binary between the seen (the written) and the heard (the spoken), but as we would expect, from precisely the literate, visual standpoint. It is not just that Stephen thinks by way of what he has read, though he does. His readerliness is part of a dominant literate worldview that puts his very presence at stake. Take, for instance, the first passage of "Proteus":

> Ineluctable modality of the visible: at least that if no more, thought through my eyes. Signatures of all things I am here to read, seaspawn and seawrack, the nearing tide, that rusting boot. Snotgreen, blue-silver, rust: coloured signs. Limits of the diaphane. But he adds: in bodies. Then he was aware of them bodies before of them coloured. How? By knocking his sconce against them, sure. (*U*, 3.1–6)

Stephen plays with his natural element (the visual) as he strolls along that element he cannot contemplate without fear: water. Framing an abstract investigation within the parameters of Aristotelian thought, Stephen analyses phenomenal apprehension. How can it be that for Aristotle, sense of the bodily existence of a thing comes before the sense of its visual appearance? "Then he was aware of them bodies before of them coloured. How?" For Stephen, visuals come first, a visuality that is thought through a long tradition as reading: "Signatures of all things I am here to read,"[6] and through his own history as a reader, here, of Aristotle. Bodies, for Stephen, are emphatically problematic: he is all mind.[7]

Stephen's idea of his own existence is somehow centrally tied to seeing. When he closes his eyes to experience the "ineluctable modality of the audible" he disappears from the world: or it disappears from him. Opening them again, he (or it) returns.

> Open your eyes now. I will. One moment. Has all vanished since? If I open and am for ever in the black adiaphane. *Basta*! I will see if I can see.
>
> See now. There all the time without you: and ever shall be, world without end. (*U*, 3.25–28)

He acknowledges that the physical presence of things does not depend on his seeing them, but when he closes his eyes, either he or the world, or both are in question. When he opens them, he and it have returned.

But for our purposes here, it is enough to note the way in which Stephen demonstrates the literate worldview: analytically, abstractly, experimentally calling on the literate philosophical tradition he has read to approach the problem of his own phenomenology. Whether the world is there—and how we can tell—is a question that would simply never be asked in an oral culture, where the world is everywhere and always evidently present. To put the world at issue is precisely the literate approach, where even one's own existence is called into question, objectified and investigated, rather than simply lived. In short, the problem with Stephen is he has read too many books, and has yet to fully discover and embrace a simple audible presence he already associates with women, and with his own mouth.

> His lips lipped and mouthed fleshless lips of air: mouth to her moomb. Oomb, allwombing tomb. His mouth moulded issuing breath, unspeeched: ooeeehah: roar of cataractic planets, globed, blazing, roaring wayawayawayawayaway. Paper. The banknotes, blast them. Old Deasy's letter. Here. Thanking you for the hospitality tear the blank end off. Turning his back to the sun he bent over far to a table of rock and scribbled words. (*U*, 3.401–407)

Stephen has met the cocklepickers, male and female, on the beach, and has inflated their appearance into various guises: "red Egyptians," "a ruffian and his strolling mort," and a "lord [and] his helpmeet." This protean transmogrification—like all the sea changes in this episode—happens through Stephen's literate ability to apply many names to the same thing. The sight of the couple brings sex—never too far away—to Stephen's mind. He casts the woman as prostitute, the man as pimp or "fancyman," yet another set of identities for the pair. Then, like the bird-girl of *A Portrait*, the gypsy woman is imaginatively transformed into the "handmaid of the moon," figure of all women. Looking at her, Stephen is moved to speech, but a speech that leads directly to writing. His lips collapse "mouth" and "womb," orality and woman, into "moomb." "Moomb," rhyming with "tomb," suggests the rest of this cognitive package: women, whose mouths and wombs mean sex and birth (that is, signal presence), for Stephen continue toward death (and writing), since that womb which gave him presence, his mother, is now dead. Immediately, he must "scribble words" and searches for paper on which to capture and represent this fundamentally auditory experience. He finds the tail end of Garrett Deasy's letter about hoof-and-mouth disease (more masculine preoccupation with mouths). The binary is set: while men (Stephen, Garrett Deasy) think and write, women *are*, and their presence is the presence of the spoken: the warm, erotic jointure of mouth and womb.

The association of women with a pre- or aliterate erotic presence may hold for the highly educated Stephen (and Joyce), but it signals a cognitive distance from the Irish as a people, since Irish women were not, in fact, less literate than men. In fact, by 1901, women from fifteen to twenty-four years of age were slightly more likely to be able to read and write than young men of the same age, with nearly everyone in those age groups basically literate: 95 percent of women, and 93 percent of men. But the level of literacy was primitive for both genders. David Fitzpatrick writes:

> By the late nineteenth century young women were marginally more likely to be literate than their male masters. For those in poor and "backward" counties such as Mayo, women overhauled men despite their even greater initial handicap, though men remained more literate for a decade or so longer. This educational triumph should not be overstated. As late as 1901, two of Ireland's 110 female publishers, booksellers, and librarians were unable to write, while a third woman could not so much as read. (Fitzpatrick, 168)

Not actually illiterate, both men and women in Ireland in the first decade of the twentieth century were about as close to it as they very well could be. Joyce's women reflect this rudimentary literacy, which points up, if anything, the foreignness of the written word to woman.[8] Molly, Milly, Martha Clifford are anything but learned, and their disassociation with literary life is central to their womanliness, a crucial part of their attraction. Bluestockings, on the other hand, are precisely unattractive; ladies of letters are "grief and kickshaws" (*U*, 3.429–30). When Bloom imagines Lizzy Twigg, whose work has found the approval of A.E., it is a slovenly picture: "No time to do her hair drinking sloppy tea with a book of poetry" (*U*, 8.332–3). And his impression is (perhaps) confirmed. Catching sight of A.E. later in the day, Bloom sees he is accompanied by a woman. "Her stockings are loose over her ankles. I detest that: so tasteless. Those literary etherial people they all are. Dreamy, cloudy, symbolistic" (*U*, 8.542–43). Literate women, caught up in the cloudy symbolism of the written, haven't time to attend to the erotics of stockings. Molly Ivors from "The Dead" seems the only positively depicted literate woman in the canon. It is she who laughs at the pompous Gabriel, and she who escapes the confines of the moribund party. But she's not pretty.[9]

Despite his material support from several talented literary women, Joyce's most misogynistic moments seem centered on the figure of the literate woman. "I hate women who know anything," he growls[10] (Ellmann, *Joyce,* 634). As if to demonstrate how alien books are to women, Joyce held that they put them in bookcases upside down (Ellmann, 463). Nora Barnacle's apparent disdain for, or at least uninterest in her husband's work, may be the source for this sharply defined binary: literate women are unattractive, even unnatural; illiterate ones desirable, partly by way of their very illiteracy.

In *Ulysses*, women's most definitive moments as oral subjects come precisely when they try to write. Martha Clifford, carrying on a flirtatious correspondence with "Henry Flower" (Bloom's alias), demonstrates in one missive an effective erotic strategy and dicey composition skills.

> Dear Henry
> I got your last letter to me and thank you very much for it. I am sorry you did not like my last letter. Why did you enclose the stamps? I am awfully angry with you. I do wish I could punish you for that. I called you naughty boy because I do not like that other world. Please tell me what is the real meaning of that word? Are you not happy in your home you poor little naughty boy? I do wish I could do something for you. Please tell me what you think of poor me. I often think of the beautiful name you have. Dear Henry, when will we meet? I think of you so often you have no idea. I have never felt myself so much drawn to a man as you. I feel so bad about. Please write me a long letter and tell me more. Remember if you do not I will punish you. So now you know what I will do to you, you naughty boy, if you do not wrote. O how I long to meet you. Henry dear, do not deny my request before my patience are exhausted. Then I will tell you all. Goodbye now, naughty darling. I have such a bad headche. today. and write *by return* to your longing
> Martha
> P.S. Do tell me what kind of perfume does your wife use. I want to know.
> XXXX
> (*U*, 5.241–59)

Writing in response to what must have been a fairly ribald letter—Bloom thinks, "No answer probably. Went too far last time" (*U*, 5.58-59)—Martha Clifford does not adopt his probably obscene vocabulary, and in fact professes ignorance about it. ("Please tell me what is the real meaning of that word?") Clearly aware that this is a game of titillation, her erotic strategies are not those of literacy; she does not try to move him through obscene words, skillful rhetoric, visualization or image. Instead, hers is a simple voice, positioning itself as unaccustomed to the writerly medium, and not very proficient at it: "I am sorry you did not like my last letter." Her errors of grammar and punctuation, run-on sentences, repetitive gush

("Dear Henry," "you naughty boy"), and simple recurring sentence structure mark this as closer to the spoken than the written, for all its enscripture. "Before my patience are exhausted," thinks the word "patience" through the sound, not the meaning, causing a plural verb to follow. That it is a howler for literates capable of reading a complex book like *Ulysses* underlines the work's willingness to laugh at women, but from a particularly literate (masculine) standpoint. We might apply to Martha's letter the postscript appended to Milly Bloom's letter to her father: "P.S. Excuse bad writing am in hurry."

All the same, Martha Clifford writes an effectively erotic missive, well attuned to Bloom's particular sexual fantasies: punishment by a strong woman, for instance. She threatens punishment explicitly twice, and once by implication: before her patience are exhausted. There is a coy innocence about the letter, a profession of being unaware of the terms of the exchange, asking about his words and why he sent her stamps, while at the same time repetitively spurring him to write more: "Please write me a long letter and tell me more," and "write *by return* to your longing." Mixed with complaint and anger are pity and concern in a maternal vein: "Are you not happy in your home you poor little naughty boy? I do wish I could do something for you." The enclosure of a pressed flower to a man calling himself Henry Flower signals both a certain intelligence—the pun of sending a flower to a Flower—and a certain limitation in woman. She sends not skillful writing, but a bit of nature. The letter sparks a reflection on "the language of flowers" in Bloom, who concludes that Martha is, "of course," "afraid of words" (*U*, 5.274). Where does this "of course" come from? From the fact that she is a woman. So far are they from literate proficiency, that Bloom, highlighting her incorrect tense, "wonders did she wrote it herself"[11] (*U*, 5.268–9).

Joyce has a close association with the erotics of letters, most famously evidenced by his 1909 correspondence with Nora Barnacle. The written word, always for Joyce charged with power, becomes specifically sexually powerful when penned in certain ways by certain women. In their status as nonwriters, women's writing counts as excess or transgression to the rule of the written. It is both writing and not writing. Its place outside the system of literate control, marked by, among other things, negligence toward punctuation, opens the written word to an erotic abandon registered materially on the body. That the "Penelope" episode was originally conceived as the transcription of letters by Molly, modeled on Nora's to Joyce (Beja, 69), points up this trajectory away from writing, through women's writing, toward orality and the erotic.

Molly the Mouth

Clearly our fullest experience of the oral within the written *Ulysses* is in Molly's monologue. All the hallmarks of orality are munificently present. Preservational, repetitive, pragmatic, situational, formulaic, unselfconscious, Molly's reflections flow uncontained, bulging and breaking a literate sentence structure, too full to bear those bonds.

> yes I think he made them a bit firmer sucking them like that so long he made me thirsty titties he calls them I had to laugh yes this one anyhow stiff the nipple gets for the least thing Ill get him to keep that up and Ill take those eggs beaten up with marsala fatten them out for him what are all those veins and things curious the way its made 2 the same in case of twins theyre supposed to represent beauty placed up there like those statues in the museum one of them pretending to hide it with her hand are they so beautiful of course compared with what a man looks like with his two bags full and his other thing hanging down out of him or sticking up at you like a hatrack (*U*, 18.535–44)

Orality's repetition is depicted as Molly thinks again and again of clothing, of kissing, and especially of men. Her review of the day links back to contain the whole of her life, from Gibraltar on, marking the conservative or mnemonic nature of oral thought, the medium of memory. Adding thought to thought, one situational memory triggers another, and these exist side by side, additive and aggregative, without hierarchy or conclusion. There is thinking here, but it is mostly the recitation of presumed knowledge, rather than the experimental urge to test what is known, as with Stephen. Molly thinks she knows that Boylan makes her breasts firmer (presumably for the long term) by sucking them, and that she can add fat specifically to her embonpoint by eating eggs in marsala, and that women have two breasts in order to suckle twins. When she considers an abstract and rather linguistic notion (breasts representing beauty) she returns the thought to specifics—the statues in the museum—and moves quickly on to thinking of men's genitalia: the abstraction is dropped.

It is difficult to quote "Penelope." Even in a very simple and direct way, it resists extrapolation. It is diffuse not concentrated, circuitous not direct, repetitive not progressive. To choose any one point at which to enter the text, in order to "prove a point" means ignoring or evading several others, all vaguely connected, that might have been used. It simply does not reduce—or reduce well—to message or argument. It sprawls, intervening by way of the oral with the literate rule of the quote. Identities merge, "he" is emphatically problematic, and, while it might be said that Molly's thought goes nowhere, she might rather ask where she ought to go?[12]

"Penelope" does, in a way, fulfill the desire of quotation. Here indeed seems to be an authentic voice, present and unmediated. But if Molly is all talk, hers is an excessive fulfillment of the oral within the written, a voice that exceeds and to some degree displaces a quotational ideal that seeks to retain the voice within bounds set by the interests of patriarchy, capitalism, and the figure of the author. While Molly has clearly entered the written, as the single voice behind the famous concluding episode of Joyce's *Ulysses,* her voice can recall to us something of a prior kind of expression: a shared mode of communication modernity has feminized and marginalized, even as it has commodified and controlled it between its inverted commas. Molly's soliloquy is hardly a revolutionary gesture. It is, after all, literature. But it can recollect us to a lost intimacy that the quote meant to replicate, and cannot.

But before we make our claims for "Penelope" too broad, we must remember one thing: Molly does read, even if she doesn't know what "metempsychosis" means.[13] In the first Bloom episode, we find she has recently finished *Ruby: The Pride of the Ring.* Donald Gifford identifies the title as a sentimental exposé of circuses, but Joyce seems to have spiced it up considerably, adding illustrations of all but naked women ("Sheet kindly lent") assailed by whips, and a plot that centers around a love affair: "Is she in love with the first fellow all the time?" Molly asks Bloom (*U,* 4.355–56). While she claims there is "nothing smutty in it" (*U,* 4.355), it seems clear that Molly's taste in reading runs to the sensational and mildly pornographic.[14] (Her asking Bloom about the plot of the book reveals his does, too.)

But they seem to diverge in what they like in an erotic text. Bloom at the Merchant's Arch, browsing for books, considers and rejects *Fair Tyrants,* by James Lovebirch, for Molly. He's read it ("Had it? Yes." *U,* 10.602), but remembers "No: she wouldn't like that much. Got her it once" (*U,* 10.605). *Sweets of Sin* is "more in her line" (606):

—All the dollarbills her husband gave her were spent in the stores on wondrous gowns and costliest frillies. For him! For Raoul!
    Yes. This. Here. Try.
—Her mouth glued on his in a luscious voluptuous kiss while his hands felt for the opulent curves inside her deshabille.
    Yes. Take this. The end.
—You are late, he spoke hoarsely, eying her with a suspicious glare.

> *The beautiful woman threw off her sabletrimmed wrap, displaying her queenly shoulders and heaving embonpoint. An imperceptible smile played round her perfect lips as she turned to him calmly.* (U, 10.608–17)

Reading these brief snatches of text, Bloom's body is affected. He begins to breathe heavily, and to fantasize. He reads again the part about the queenly woman turning on the man. This passage in particular—we know he likes "fair tyrants"—seems to impel him to a kind of swoon, but an ambiguous one. This might be the transport of a succumbing female:

> Warmth showered gently over him, cowing his flesh. Flesh yielded amply amid rumpled clothes: whites of eyes swooning up. His nostrils arched themselves for prey. Melting breast ointments (*for him! for Raoul!*). Armpits' oniony sweat. Fishgluey slime (*her heaving embonpoint!*). Feel! Press! Chrished! Sulphur dung of lions! (U, 10.619–23)

Bloom seems to be achieving a kind of orgasmic identification with the heroine of the piece. His flesh is "cowed" (feminized) and "yields." What prey his nostrils arch themselves for is ambiguous. Does he as aggressor sniff for prey, or do they arch themselves to mark *him* as prey? Smells come: ointments, sweat, the salty, fishy smell of vaginal moisture, all somatic responses to the arousal played out on three levels: in the scene in *Sweets of Sin*, in the scene in Bloom's text-generated fantasy, and in the bookstall at the Merchants' Arch. Who is to feel whom, who press whom? Language itself begins to swoon: "crished" seems to mark intercourse between "crushed" and any number of words employing an *i*: the proximate "fishgluey slime," perhaps.

Bloom's reading of *Sweets of Sin*, marked as a feminized reading, further identifies female literacy as still largely oral: suggestible, subjective, out of control, acritical. Women's susceptibility and physical weakness are, as Kate Flint has demonstrated, historically used as legitimation for a rigourous control of their reading. (Whether or not one could allow young girls to read *Ulysses* was the acid test of acceptability in the book's obscenity trial.) A feminized Bloom is clearly not in control of his response to *Sweets of Sin*, and his powerful somatic reaction is marked specifically as a loss of masculinity. He becomes a woman and a weak reader at the same moment. He is not left, however, as May Dedalus is, with only what the book gives him, reader relegated to simple iteration, though he does repeat some phrases ("For Raoul!"). His response constitutes both a repetition and extension of the text. The language of the book (*Sweets of Sin*) leaks into the language of Bloom's mind (the language of *Ulysses*) and the two interact. "Opulent curves inside her deshabille," becomes "Flesh . . . amid rumpled clothes." The presence—in an otherwise adverbless context—of "hoarsely" and "calmly" engenders further adverbs in Bloom's mutated repetition: "gently" and "amply." The sable in the passage may nudge forward Bloom's (or *Ulysses*') notion of prey, and perhaps of the even more inexplicable textual riff "sulphur dung of lions!" (A hangover from *Ruby, Pride of the Ring*?) Further, this textuality may be informed by more than merely what Bloom reads: the choice of the verb "arched" in "arched for prey" and the "oniony" of "oniony sweat" may owe something to the onion smell of the proprietor's breath at the Merchants' Arch: the physical world. Infected by text and context, this passage will continue to circulate and transmogrify as it surfaces throughout the remainder of Bloom's day.[15]

In reading *Sweets of Sin,* Bloom transgresses far more than his gender identity. Engaging on a somatic, feminized level with the text he reads, he has broken that boundary between between reader and thing read on which the modern, masculine, literate identity depends. Pornographic prose—indeed any prose that can so powerfully sway us—ignores or evades the modern split between subject and object, allowing infection, invasion, contamination, illicit exchange. This, more than the denigration of pleasure, may be why pornography has been so strictly censored: it threatens our sense of ourselves as moderns.

In the United States at least, words are no longer thought to have this power. Legally, text can no longer count as obscene or pornographic, precisely because it is assumed to carry with it a critical awareness (Nead, 97). According to the 1986 Meese Committee, photographic representations alone trigger the erotic "reflex action" that so threatens our equilibrium: more evidence that the literate subject, now more than ever, guarantees modernity's self-control. And so the censorship debate moves on to photographers like Robert Mapplethorpe. Writers and writing, presumably, can no longer get to us this way. *Ulysses,* then, is no longer obscene *or* emetic: it presumably cannot affect us in such a direct way as to move our bodies, evading our minds.

Quotation, that system of containment whereby modernity can be certain of that mind, undergoes a radical threat as *Ulysses* shows *Sweets of Sin* subverting the straight path of discourse. This may indeed be the sweetest sin of all, and the one *Ulysses* finds most delicious. This reading is felt in the body, and as such is deeply dangerous.[16] *Ulysses* provides an evasive strategy with two faces: first, a resistant residual orality associated with erotics and with women; then, a feminine literacy that redeploys the erotic as a means of overturning the modern reader's position. The first employs ignorance ("illiteracy") in the cause of difference; the second exploits the body's vulnerabilities. The next and final chapter will move these transgressions within the Joyce text outward, tracing the relationship between Joyce's words and their most passionate readers: Joyceans. For, to read Joyce's prose is to stand with Bloom in the Merchants Arch: on one hand, scrupulously, properly in control; on the other: swooning, crished.

7

Joyce and the Joyceans

Take a book, and you will find it offering, opening itself. It is this openness of the book which I find so moving. A book is not shut in by its contours, is not walled-up as a fortress. It asks nothing better than to exist outside itself, or to let you exist in it. In short, the extraordinary fact in the case of a book is the falling away of the barriers between you and it.

Georges Poulet, "Criticism and Interiority"

So far, this book has been concerned with writing and speaking. It has described the way in which quotation, a written form, attempts to capture and preserve the authentic spoken word. It has traced a masculine quotational structure of separation, contestation, and property enacted through a concern for style and the author. It has sketched a quotational necessity in modernity's confrontation with the past, and an oral, feminine resistance to quotation's power. So far, modern citation has had most to do with what might be called *expressive* modes: writing, speaking, and the ways in which quotation constructs certain versions of them. However, quotation does not exist purely as an expressive, writerly set of ideas. As the previous chapter has found in Bloom's encounter with *Sweets of Sin*, quotation holds in its heart a deep anxiety about *reception*: about reading. Quotation has impressed our notion of reading with a dominant modern writerliness. One reads in control, to control. Reading is a struggle readers must win.

Reading is the central problem for quotation. As a system of fragmentation and possession, violence and control, the modern citational process is primarily thought of as a writerly one: what writers must do (to readings) to establish their places in discourse. (There is an urgent, identificatory necessity in this "must.") In this dynamic, the status of the read, and the fact that the author must, in some way and to some degree, *give himself over* to the reading, worries a citational structure intent on a means of *gaining oneself* by way of ownership and accountability. Somehow, readers must be sensitive to the read, but must at the same time be wary, must keep their distance. Influence generates "anxiety."[1]

Against Reading

Reading, then, has sunk beneath a dominant narrative of writing. Take, as token, this introductory passage from a popular composition anthology.

> Reading involves a fair measure of push and shove. You make your mark on a book and it makes its mark on you. Reading is not simply a matter of hanging back and waiting for a piece, or its author, to tell you what the writing has to say. In fact, one of the difficult things about reading is that the pages before you will begin to speak only when the authors are silent and you begin to speak in their place, sometimes for them, doing their work, continuing their projects, and sometimes for yourself, following your own agenda. This is an unusual way to talk about reading, we know. (Bartholomae and Petrosky, 1)

This from a work intended to produce writers and writing; it is not surprising to see a promotion of readerly rigor, of reading in such a way as to write. The clear divergence between *him*, "the author," and the reader's "own agenda" re-marks the subjective split quotation institutes. Even if the book will "make its mark on you," this might almost suggest that it will help define you as yourself: reading marks you with a distinguishing line. At any rate, what the book does to the reader is submerged in what the reader will do to the book.

The casual practice of referring to authors as the possessions of their readers rises to mind here: one reads one's Shakespeare, one's Dante, one's Joyce. You are a reader, and these readings belong to you, marking your identity as a member of a literate culture, a member of the club of the West. P. G. Wodehouse's joke, in which Bertie Wooster replies to the compliment, "Bertie, you know your Shelley," with "Oh, am I?" demonstrates just this point: readerly possession funds identity.

Whether this is an "unusual" way to think about reading seems questionable. The Anglo-American critical tradition has embraced a rigorous, self-assertive readerliness at least since F. R. Leavis's bracing perorations of the 1930s.[2] Many contemporary critics and theorists, uncomfortable heirs of Leavis, follow in rigor if not in specific sentiment *Scrutiny*'s agenda in cobbling literature to theory in the subordinate role of the quoted: as exemplar, as demonstration of a preexistent theoretical truth. Life force was what mattered in Leavis's view, and life force was what he found. Less aggressive notions of reading, then and now, are read as passive, personal, idiosyncratic, and self-indulgent,[3] despite articulate calls for a notion of reading that is not *that*.[4] When James Boswell notes that Samuel Johnson would seize "at once what was valuable in any book, without submitting to the labour of perusing it from beginning to end" (Boswell, 17), he means it as a compliment.

Bartholomae and Petrosky's most proximate influence would seem to be Roland Barthes and reader reception criticism in general. Following the view articulated in "The Death of the Author" (1966) that "The real writer is the reader," these editors take up (and, properly, extend) the distinction Barthes elaborates in *S/Z* (1970) between the readerly and the writerly. Barthes writes,

> Our literature is characterized by the pitiless divorce which the literary institution maintains between the producer of the text and its user, between its owner and its customer, between its author and its reader. This reader is thereby plunged into a kind of idleness—he is intransitive; he is, in short, *serious:* instead of functioning himself, instead of gaining access to the magic of the signifier, to the pleasure of writing, he is left with no more than the poor freedom either to accept or reject the text. (Barthes, 4)

Barthes describes the typology this separation makes available. Readerly texts are easy enough to find: they are the commodified "classics" on sale everywhere. They can be read, that is, consumed, but not written (written over, or rewritten by the reader). Writerly texts, at the other extreme, exist in no completed material form. Since the writerly text is productive, not representative, it can have no criticism *about* it, which, "once produced, would mix with it" (Barthes, 5). Between the too, too solid readerly classic and the almost mystical, dynamic writerly, Barthes lays out a range of texts, plotted according to what Barthes sees as Nietzsche's style of interpretation: not to reduce a text to the monovocal meaning of representation, but to "appreciate what *plural* constitutes it" (Barthes, 5).

What precisely drops out of this equation is reading, which has been consigned to a passive, middle-class practice of consumption: May Daedalus's escapism. Damned as the lazy handmaiden of the commodified author, reading is rewritten into a hegemony of the writerly reader, who will take action to produce a fully mobile, plural textuality. To read is to engage in a limited, impoverished signification, bogged in the muck of culture's repetitive representations. It is clearly writing that sets one free. "Where can we find [writerly texts]?" Barthes asks. "Certainly not in reading . . ." (Barthes, 5).

Writing counts for more, even among those who are most passionately concerned with reading. When Paul de Man and Jacques Derrida met in 1966, both were reading Rousseau. Later asked to comment of their different ways with a text, de Man said,

> My starting point . . . is not philosophical but basically philological, and for that reason didactical, text-oriented. Therefore, I have a tendency to put upon texts an inherent authority, which is stronger, I think, than Derrida is willing to put on them. . . . The difference is that Derrida's text is so brilliant, so incisive, so strong, that whatever happens in Derrida, it happens between him and his own text. He doesn't need Rousseau, he doesn't need anybody else; I do need them very badly because I never had an idea of my own, it was always through a text, through the critical examination of a text . . . I am a philologist and not a philosopher. . . . (*The Resistance to Theory,* 118)

Philosophers, then, are active, strong, independent of what they read, without "needs," generating their own discourse, having their own ideas. Philologists, on the other hand, are passive, tied to the text, dependent though critical, without ideas of "their own." De Man depicts himself as reader, Derrida as writer.

Antoine Compagnon follows this reader/writer opposition more specifically into the field of citation. Thinking about reading and citation, Compagnon articulates the subordination of the former under the writerly control of the latter. Underlining is the start of it all.

> Le soulignement en lecture est l'épreuve préliminaire de la citation (et de l'écriture), un repérage visuel, materiel, qui institue mon droit de regard sur le texte. Telle une reconnaissance militaire, il pose des jalons, des repaires surcharges de sens, ou de valeur; il surimpose une nouvelle ponctuation au texte, faite au rythme de ma lecture: ce sont les pointilles suivant lesquels je découperai plus tard. Toute citation est d'abord une lecture—de manière équivalente, toute lecture, comme soulignement, est une citation. (Compagnon, 21)

Underlining is the preliminary proof of citation (and of writing), a visual, material track which institutes the right of my gaze on the text. Like a military reconnaissance, the underline stakes out the territory, the magazines of supercharged meaning or value. It superimposes a new punctuation on the text, formed by the rhythm of my reading: these are the dotted lines along which I will later cut. All citation is just such a reading—and, in the same manner, all reading, like underlining, is citation in this way.

For Compagnon, to read *is* to write, to have already and immediately separated, selected, fragmented, written over the reading. The citational economy, for him, happens in the moment of reading, and there is no reading that does not enact precisely this kind of ex*cite*d violence on a text. His is a vision of an unimpeachable reader, proof against a text that cannot subvert his position of authority over it. Caught forever in Compagnon's net of signification, the text begins to approach the status of chaotic nature: a scene to be tamed, and, if not brought in line with an unquestionable Truth, at least brought in line with Compagnon's version, which somehow preexists and lies over it.

This line of thinking about the relationship between the reader and the read has led to a logical enough theoretical reductio ad absurdum: Stanley Fish's questioning of the existence of any object of reading at all.[5] Demonstrating well the way in which the modern writerly dynamic of quotational control has continued to thrive even within a horizon of thinking suspicious of control on other levels,[6] Compagnon's depiction of citation's liaison with writerly control continues a tradition of readerly suppression, a suppression intimately tied to the modern autonomous subject.

Part of the problem modernity has with any reading that does not engender a writing (either closed and critical or open and plural) is that such a reading is not visible: there is no underline, no mark by which to represent that an eye has passed here. If one does not *quote* the text (apply the pencil or highlighter), in what way can we know it has been read? Reading that does not incite the reading voice to speak, to interpret, to paraphrase, to sum—that is, to write—cannot easily be seen within a structure built on a writerly expectation. Modern citation, the rule of the writerly within reading, abandons or ignores readerly influences that are not accounted for in citation's economy of separation.

What then could lie beyond modernity's citation? Precisely, reading. Reading that demonstrates but does not fret over a continuity of voice and method with its object of study. Reading that blurs the distinction between readerly and authorial subjectivities.[7] And this must be a continuity that is, precisely, not irony, parody, or impersonation, for those ultramodernist modes serve only to emphasize an authorial rewriting, a subjectival separation, the control of the ironic stance.⁸ Nor can this be a continuity of adoration, a repetition or emulation engendered by admiration, for that sort of a continuity also retraces the separation of text and reader, merely reversing the citational dominance. Laying aside reverence and ridicule alike, if reading is to take on a new form as postmodern literacy, it must begin to understand itself as continuous with its object, dwelling in it rather than surveying it from on high. Joyce scholarship often exhibits this kind of continuity, but it has also worked hard to explain it away.

Under the Influence: Joyce and the Joyceans

Within the story of the "author," the notion of influence has achieved a qualified acceptability. Joyce's "creative" inheritors are many and respected "in their own right": Samuel Beckett, William Faulkner, Flann O'Brien. There is a moment, however, for each of these, when his work must be proclaimed his own, even as Joyce's sources are identified and their transmutation (by him) traced.⁹ But a recognition that, within the fabric and fiber of their text, lies that of another, is clearly, though a problem, less of a problem among writers than it is among critics, where a notion of scientific distance is, at least since Matthew Arnold's call for disinterestedness and a free play of the mind, a requirement. Influence is all very well *among writers,* who may share certain "universal" topics or genres, or *among critics,* who may share a methodology, but to breach these discrete groupings makes for illicit fraternization. Any jointure in methods, ideas, or style between a critic and his object of study is a problem of an entirely different order than that between critics or between writers. Critics, far more than writers, must remain proof against the language they study, must read to write in ways that fend off the threat of subjectivities commingling. To speak with the voice of one's object is to "lose oneself," specifically, as a critic.

The necessity for this distinction between literature and criticism is the initial move of René Wellek and Austin Warren's 1942 *Theory of Literature.*

> We must first make a distinction between literature and literary study. The two are distinct activities: one is creative, an art; the other, if not precisely a science, is a species of knowledge or of learning.... the task of the student is completely distinct [from that of the creative writer]. He must translate his experience of literature into intellectual terms, assimilate it to a coherent scheme which must be rational if it is to be knowledge. (Wellek and Warren, 15)

Paradoxically, then, what (this) criticism precisely must *not* do, is read. Rather, it must write over the reading: "translate," and "assimilate" it into "coherence." The only other options Wellek and Warren suggest are either a "second creation," that is, a "needless duplication or, at most, the translation of one work of art into another, usually inferior" (Wellek and Warren, 15), or the abandonment of interpretation altogether, to "private indulgence" (Wellek and Warren, 15). The possibility of readerly continuity with an object of study that would not forestall an active engagement with the text, though perhaps a less "scientific" one, is not considered. Yet such continuity is readable all over the tradition of literary criticism, a sweeping agreement between critic and text that, first and foremost, this text is worth reading and criticizing in a disciplined way: is, indeed, literature.

Within the Joycean critical canon, more specific agreements and continuities exist. Long struggling to escape Joyce's seductive language, Joyceans have tended to locate and contain their quotational uneasiness in Joyce-the-man. To exorcise James Joyce's influence, to truly bury Joyce, would end his threat to the genre of writing most wedded to the quotational ideal: criticism. Joyce's Zurich gravesite is much visited, especially by his critics.[10] But what is clearer than ever, is how Joyce continues to generate criticism—and "his kind" of criticism—at an astonishing rate.

Since early in 1941, the point at which it is generally understood James Joyce ceased participating in the criticism surrounding his works, Joyce as an interpretive project has grown enormously, earning him the title "God's gift to English Departments" (Johnston). A bibliography completed by Robert Deming to cover Joyce criticism prior to 1973 has over 5,500 entries and has been both extensively amended through that date and much augmented after it. More recently, Geert Lernout tells us that "[Joyce's] reputation keeps growing. . . . The result is an absolutely daunting number of books, articles, and reviews that was at the last count reaching the ten thousand mark" (Lernout, 21). The *Arts and Humanities Citation Index* for 1988 showed Joyce citation totals well ahead of any other twentieth-century author, critic, scientist, or philosopher. He was mentioned more that year than Wittgenstein, Kuhn, Derrida, or Foucault. More recently, *The Chronicle of Higher Education* lists Joyce entries in the 1996 *MLA Bibliography* as second in number only to Shakespeare's. It is clear that Joyce has been an immensely successful generator of critical prose.

His role in initiating and guiding the critical response to his work has long been acknowledged, but it has been carefully located only among those friends and contemporaries he could affect personally. Lernout, for instance, admits that

> The history of Joyce criticism starts with the author himself. Few modern writers have been so aware as Joyce was of the importance of criticism for the reception of his later and more difficult novels, and he personally inspired and supervised almost all of the major studies on his work that were published during his lifetime. (Lernout, 21)

Lernout carefully marks a line underneath Joyce criticism at the point of Joyce's death, citing Harry Levin's 1941 *James Joyce: A Critical Introduction* as the first example of a work "independent of Joyce's personal involvement."

A new age of critical objectivity, of freedom from the man himself, must have been particularly welcome in a critical canon that had been experiencing author trouble for some time. Until Richard Ellmann's 1959 biography, Joyce's readers, especially after *A Portrait* arrived, were faced with the difficulty of ascertaining precisely where the "real life" of James Joyce existed in his quasi-autobiographical texts, and what could be chalked up to creative mutation: to art. In the New Critical context of the 1950s, the problem of Joyce's biographical presence in his work was disturbing for scholars interested in establishing him as an academic topic of study.[11]

Oddly, this critical difficulty already existed in the fiction itself, set out by Joyce in *Ulysses*. In the "Scylla and Charybdis" episode, Stephen explicates Shakespeare's works *a clef,* insisting on a biographical reading, while A.E. splutters, "But this prying into the family life of a great man. . . . Interesting only to the parish clerk. I mean, we have the plays" (*U*, 155). With A.E.—at least as Joyce depicts him—New Criticism sought to shear the writer and his times away from the work. Stephen Dedalus, the fictive persona of Joyce within his works, insists on the biographical.

In 1964, Peter Speilberg assesses the Joyce-the-man difficulty from the pages of the newly established *James Joyce Quarterly.*

> The problem of Joyce biography has always been a sticky one. Even critics and biographers of great fame and ability have had much trouble in keeping apart James Joyce and Joyce's fictional *Doppelganger,* Stephen Dedalus. The temptation to see autobiographical material in the *Bildungsroman, A Portrait of the Artist as a Young Man,* and in *Ulysses* is understandable, but regrettable since it leads towards confusion. Because of this merging, the real has become fictional, and the fictional has become glued so tightly to the truth that separation of the two now seems impossible without tearing the print from the page and the skin from the flesh. (Speilberg, 42)

And so it was with great relief that Joyceans greeted the publication of a definitive biography of Joyce in 1959, a biography written not by a suggestible friend of Joyce's, as Herbert Gorman's 1939 effort had been, but by Richard Ellmann, a professional scholar, a good reader, an able historian: someone who had never met James Joyce.[12] By delineating precisely that which was "Joyce himself" and that which was Joyce's creation, criticism could sleep more easily knowing the boundary between art and life (and their ability to separate them out) to be safe.

Pioneer Joycean Bernard Benstock offered a retrospective on the discipline from the vantage point of 1966, proclaiming just this liberation: that Joyce's power to control his critics was finally at an end. That Joyce was, in fact, really and truly dead.

> Many of Joyce's contemporaries are now dead, both the disciples who sat at the Master's feet and the detractors who ran afoul of his ego and his pen, and a new generation of writers has grown up with [Richard] Ellmann's sort of objectivity. . . . Once hailed as a godsend to Ph.D. candidates, Joyce is more the property of the professional scholars and critics today, the amateurs doing well to find an easier source for their academic sinecures. With one shift digging into the notes and sources, another collating facts, figures, and symbols on the surface, while a third labors on loftier reaches to offer overall pronouncements, productivity is at a record high, and Joyce, the man, the work, and reputation, has now evolved into Joyce, the Industry. (Benstock, 211–12)

At first, it seems clear what the understood relationship between Joyce and his critics is to be: Joyce, no longer a man, is the "property" of his now "professional scholars," who, like Richard Ellmann, will provide "objective" work on him, his work, and his reputation. Joyce, the critical mover, and certainly Joyce the man, have been evaded and "Joyce" can be comfortably commodified, the product of another late capitalist industry.

Yet, even at the moment independence is declared, we sense Joyce everywhere: in the religious metaphor of master and disciple applied to the artist and his (ultimately treacherous) friends, a metaphor carried forward as Joyce becomes a "godsend" to Ph.D. candidates. That particular imposition of the artistic over the religious is a trick of James Joyce's. As is the facetious diminishment of the religious to secular purposes, as Ph.D. candidates receive gifts sent from God. This collapsing of the sacred and profane smacks of Stephen Dedalus, picking his nose and thinking of Aristotle, or

Leopold Bloom, parsing the crucifix's "I.N.R.I." as "iron nails run in" (he is quoting Molly). In the extended metaphor of the mine (surely suggestive of that prior Daedalus's labyrinth) that orders the passage, we can sense a particularly Joycean device, and one that T. S. Eliot pointed out in his 1923 essay in the *Dial*, "*Ulysses:* Order and Myth." The concomitant metaphors of the family ("generations") and of evolution ("Joyce has now evolved") suggest what has been identified as Joyce's concern for the broadness of time and change, but always as it concerns the human.

Perhaps the most Joycean characteristic of the passage is its emphasis on the value of the objective, which recalls to us Joyce's early valorization and supremely successful articulation of realism's aesthetic of objectivity: what he called, under the influence of Henrik Ibsen, "lofty, impersonal power." It would, of course, be specious to claim that the objective is particular to Joyce or indeed to realism as a literary goal. But what we can begin to trace is the way in which the reader, especially of Joyce's early work, is positioned as removed observer, viewing the scene of a phenomenon he or she is indifferently presented with *as phenomenon*. Joyce is away, paring his fingernails.

It is no surprise, then, that Joyce's closest and most interested readers would take most seriously the dictates of his fiction, which can be seen to produce, by way of its narrative perspective, just this variety of modern critic. These dictates, however, must never be seen as such, for their very condition of existence is that they not be seen as critical dictation. The modern critic must be free to look in precisely the same way the artist must be free, "to discover the mode of life or of art whereby . . . spirit could express itself in unfettered freedom" (Joyce, *A Portrait*, 246). There is a fundamental ambiguity in the term "Joycean." It signifies not only one who reads Joyce professionally, but that which is proper to Joyce, and belongs to him.[13]

Joyce's style, like all style presumably a guarantor of the singular speaker within language, is perhaps an even more seductive point of slippage between the writer and his critics. Here, at the point where the sanctity of authorial ownership ought to be most respected, we can occasionally read an illicit stylistic sharing of the kind to which Joyce himself confessed. Critical practice's preoccupation with style, a particularly obsessive one, finds transgression of its rules very sweet; again, the high moderns tutor us. As Donald Marshall asks, "the fascination must be a fascination of style: how could anyone learn to talk this way? The glimpsed prospect, the promised land is the possibility that . . . I too may learn to talk like this" (Marshall, xvi). Criticism learns not only what to talk about from its object: indeed, it learns how to talk.

Here, for example, is Hugh Kenner on the "Sirens" episode of *Ulysses:*

Yet a sceptical impatience breaks through such effects, especially through that trio of sonorous Blooms, three left-hand chords barrumed by a barroom pianist:

	went
BLOOM	soft
BLOOM	I feel so lonely
BLOOM	

It is to the barroom order of virtuosity that the episode repeatedly reverts, fingers vamping the easy trill and boom, untrained voices treating themselves to the fellowship of close harmony, comfortable standby words and tunes, the worn fragments of familiar acoustic junk. Correspondingly, Joyce has set the episode on the north bank of the Liffey, a place of junkshops and pawnshops prating of 'antiques,' stagnant rooms to which have drifted brass bedsteads, fenders, framed patriotic pictures, caskets, broken cornets, lamps with statuette bases—cast off splendours; Dublin's Sargasso Sea. (Kenner, "*Ulysses,*" 87)

This is the voice of a delicious submission to Joyce's style, the smell of whom is everywhere about it: the pun, the typographical effect, the breadth of expression, the evocation of a tawdry Dublin scene not by quoting it (from Joyce), but in Kenner's "own" words.[14] This voice continues as much as it analyzes Joyce's voice, Joyce's scene, Joyce's right to speak in a certain way. Such pleasure in Joyce's text is usually deeply repressed. To whom, then, shall we say this belongs? Whose, for instance, the mannerism of a jumbled catalogue, finally named in collectivity? We find it above signed by the name of Hugh Kenner, and the title—identical to its object—of *Ulysses.* ("Cast off splendors." "Dublin's Sargasso Sea.") And we find it, too, signed by James Joyce.

Broken hoops on the shore; at the land a maze of dark cunning nets; farther away chalkscrawled backdoors and on the higher beach a dryingline with two crucified shirts. Ringsend: wigwams of brown steersmen and master mariners. Human shells. (*U,* 41)

Eleven years after *Ulysses,* Kenner claims just such stylistic continuity as a mark of critical greatness. In his introduction to the 1991 edition of Edmund Wilson's *Axel's Castle,* Kenner writes of Wilson's Yeatsian prose, "one mark of a great critic is a cunning susceptibility to the procedures of what he is writing about" (Kenner, introduction, xv). But with the word "cunning," Kenner reasserts the critical distance central to modern criticism. This is one smart strategy among others that may be taken up or left alone, not a condition of critical production.

Are We Now Postmodern Critics?

All this suggests more intimacy between critics and their objects of study than the quotational system sanctions. When critical practice demonstrates a transgressive melding of method or style, this breach of quotational separation is intentionalized or ignored, and a declaration of independence made. For Joyceans, the denial itself demonstrates a continuity it attempts to reject. Caught in its own readerliness, unable wholly to fulfill the writerly duties of quotational criticism, the uneasy modern critic lives out an ambiguity latent within his attempt to fend off his object: he struggles to keep it at a safe distance, even as it sustains him as food.

Have we now exceeded this relation with our reading? Now, here, in our presumed postmodernity, have we—and especially we Joyceans—surpassed (or perhaps merely given up on) the tense dynamic of the subject/object split, always so difficult to make good on, but always so central to our notions of ourselves as knowers, as writers, as thinkers, as professionals? (I include myself in the category "Joycean." I have now written, and you have now read, my book on Joyce.) If we are postmodern critics, we might expect to see everywhere a new kind of criticism; one that feels itself continuous with Joyce's language, deriving not authority but lexicon from it, generating not more modern metanarrative, but a careless kind of continuity. (At least, one that does not care about quotation.) Further, to count as a new dispensation, this kind of criticism would have to be more than merely tolerated institutionally, but assumed, affirmed, valorized, rewarded. Is that what we see?

Most definitely not. Joyce books of the past ten years describe and legitimate their various methods according to those (presumably extra-Joycean) theoretical commitments they have made and then understand themselves to be applying to the text. Indeed, working out methodological grounds to apply to the Joyce text remains the standard task of a first chapter (as in this book). The question of Joyce's influence on Joyceans' methods insistently fails to arise. The quintessentially modern subject/object split remains firmly in place, all the more powerful because not stated, but assumed.

Poststructuralism's calling into question of the modern critic seems not to have affected even the poststructural critical approach, which might be said—indeed has been said—to have enacted an ever-more sophisticated mastery over its objects of study, even as it derides the notion of mastery.

(And it strikes me that this is a peculiarly Derridean observation.) For example, Claudette Sartiliot's *Citation and Modernity* (1993) remains more proof against Joyce's language (though not Derrida's) than does Hugh Kenner's work from an earlier, more self-consciously modern critical era. Since Derrida has celebrated the way his critical thinking has been shaped by *Finnegans Wake*, the Sartiliot work might be said to be continuous after all, but at no point does Sartiliot point this out, or seem interested in it.

Postmodernity, for Joyce criticism, is something with which *Joyce* and the Joyce text may or may not have had something to do, depending on your critical view, but the *Joycean's* position remains firmly modern. And how could it be otherwise, in a modern academy that can only affirm the production of language as quotational? The book you have just read would not have been published if it did not count as new and original work, and if it did not quote Joyce and his critics in a carefully scholarly way, establishing a progressive, masterful, distinct viewpoint. Postmodernity today may count as little more than a new area of departmental coverage commodified into another course offering the up-to-date (that is, modern) university can supply. Criticism's chances for substantive change depend on its ability to revise its constituting rhetoric, but in an era when the humanities are under seige from conservative critics and downsizing deans, this seems an unlikely moment to see such a shift. Now more than ever, scholarship needs its most powerful and recognizable legitimating narratives, quotation and its claims first among them.

If modern citation's power erodes (and I believe it does), it is due not to an academic awareness of modernity's demise, but to a broader and longer-term cultural shift away from the literate episteme that forms the condition of its existence. Quotation's waning proceeds by way of the electronic media's ability to reproduce and circulate text outside of quotational restriction, by way of the increasing hegemony of visual image over textual word, and by way of our return to (some of the characteristics of) oral culture. Just as the printing press and Roman type instituted the conditions for quotation's foundation, the telephone, television, radio, personal computer, and Internet may put in place the conditions of its collapse. We stand on the verge of a new dispensation of language, of selves, of history, and of culture at large. Somehow, James Joyce is already there.

Notes

Chapter 1

1. That more current criticism shares these quotational goals of control and unification, even when employing alternate approaches to intertextuality, is demonstrated by M. Keith Booker's Bakhtinian work *Joyce, Bakhtin, and the Literary Tradition*. Booker's introduction echoes the cartographical, ordering *view* of earlier *Wake* criticism, writing, "When viewed through the optic of Bakhtin's theories of the novel, for example, seemingly unruly and disjointed works ranging from *Gargantua and Pantagruel*, to *Tristram Shandy*, to *Moby-Dick*, to *Ulysses*, to *Gravity's Rainbow* take on a new coherence of structure, purpose, and genre" (Booker, 7).

Chapter 2

1. See Kurt Spellmeyer's "The Essay in the Academy," 262–75.

2. The notion of citation either as supplementary ornament or forensic appeal to authority is dominant from classical rhetoric to the present day. Herman Meyer, for instance, writes a "poetics" of quotation in 1968, one year after Paul Boller's "politics." See Herman Meyer's *Poetics of Quotation* and Paul Boller's *Quotesmanship*.

3. Called so by Gerard Genette in his *Palimpsests*.

4. Compagnon's subject is not, however, that subject: the modern, bordered, autonomous, integrated individual. For him the term means something more like "position in language." As an historian of citation, Compagnon describes the varied forms and functions of repetition from classicism to the modern age, but is interested neither in tying its development to that of the modern individual, as I am, nor in critiquing a bordered economy of language.

5. Samuel Johnson, in affixing citational examples to many of his dictionary's terms, recognized the violence done them: "The examples thus mutilated are no longer to be considered as conveying the sentiments or doctrine of their authors; . . . the general tendency of the sentence may be changed; the divine may desert his tenets, or the philosopher his system" (Johnson, 117). Thomas Mallon traces the way in which dictionaries, resistant to author function, are most commonly and imperturbably plagiarized (Mallon, 11–12).

6. This node of associations moves directly into the gender binary. One of portraiture's favored poses for female subjects is to represent them reading. Read-

ing, an enigma anyway, is associated with the passive and equally enigmatic feminine. See Kate Flint's *The Woman Reader*.

7. See Hazard Adams and Leroy Searle's *Critical Theory since 1965*, 728–32. Interest is indicated by a spate of "subjectivity" books and anthologies such as Jennifer Birkett and Elizabeth Harvey's *Determined Women* (1991); Julian Henriques et al.'s *Changing the Subject* (1984); Carole Satamurti's *Changing the Subject* (1990); Paul Smith's *Discerning the Subject* (1988); Eduardo Cadava, Peter Connor, and Jean-Luc Nancy's *Who Comes After the Subject?* (1991); Anthony Cascardi's *The Subject of Modernity* (1992); and Charles Taylor's two contributions, *The Sources of the Self* and *The Ethics of Authenticity* (1989 and 1991, respectively). Margot Norris's *Penelope's Web* (1992) rather shockingly brings back the intentional authorial Joyce, calling herself "theoretically retrograde" for doing so.

8. Maud Ellmann's *The Poetics of Impersonality* describes the efforts T. S. Eliot and Ezra Pound made to efface the personality, and the way in which it insistently returns.

9. See Richard H. Rouse and Mary A. Rouse's "*Statim invenire:* Schools, Preachers, and New Attitudes to the Page," in *Renaissance and Renewal in the Twelfth Century* (Cambridge: Harvard University Press, 1982), which describes twelfth century practices of citation, complete with a rudimentary quotation mark and the expressed concern that it be used, "lest you be led to mistake Cassiodorus for Augustine or Jerome, or the glossator for an expositor, a matter in which we have seen, not just the unlettered, but very learned readers fall into error" (Rouse and Rouse, 209, cited from Ignatius Brady's "The Rubrics of Peter Lombard's Sentences," *Pier Lombardo* 6 [1962]: 10–11).

10. See Roland Bainton's "The Bible in the Reformation," in *The Cambridge History of the Bible*, ed. S. L. Greenslade (Cambridge: Cambridge University Press, 1978) for a detailed description of the fight over the spirit and the letter of biblical meaning.

11. Shakespeare's modern construction of the exchange in *The Merchant of Venice* 1.3.

12. For more on this practice, see Harry Ransom's *The First Copyright Statute*.

13. See Margot Norris's discussion of this legal point in *Penelope's Web*, 33–34, and note 4.

14. For a consideration of the difficulties inherent in maintaining a sense of the original when work is reproduced, see Walter Benjamin's landmark essay "The Work of Art in the Age of Mechanical Reproduction" in *Illuminations* and a work that derives from it, Rosalind Krauss's *The Originality of the Avant-Garde and Other Modernist Myths*.

15. Editions of Augustine's *Confessions* routinely advertise the work as "the greatest spiritual autobiography of all time" (jacket blurb, 1960 Doubleday edition).

16. The precise repetition of words, or "ritualistic repetition" as linguistic anthropology terms it, exists and serves many purposes in an oral (nonquotational)

culture. However, this precise repetition is linked most often to the magical or spiritual, the unseen, and not traditionally truthful discourse. See Ong, 35.

17. For instance, in A. G. Rigg's *The English Language*, which ferries the inverted comma back far beyond its inception in the early sixteenth century to Old English and the Latin Vulgate.

18. See Walter Ong's *Orality and Literacy*, especially chapter four, "Writing Re-Structures Consciousness." Also, Elizabeth Eisenstein's *The Printing Press as an Agent of Change* and her *The Print Revolution in Early Modern Europe*.

19. Copyright law has seized the formal recognition of the verbatim as its central guide in judging cases of plagiarism. Thomas Mallon identifies this sense of the words themselves as marking ownership coming into the modern sensibility with Alexander Pope (Mallon, 8).

20. Western means of bordering the individual through punctuation is of global concern. Take, for example, how Japan adopted the quotation mark. Western grammarians had been suggesting to the Japanese throughout the eighteenth century that they employ western forms of punctuation. Nannette Twine relates that "the real impetus for the adoption of European-style punctuation, however, came from novelists who produced the various schools of modern fiction. . . . Through their efforts the practice of punctuating texts became well established and later spread outside the realm of fiction to other areas of written Japanese." See Nannette Twine's "The Adoption of Punctuation in Japanese Script," in *Visible Language* 18, no. 3 (summer 1984): 229. The repercussions of this on the Japanese self-image have yet to be traced.

21. See *Murray's English Grammar*, 117.

Chapter 3

1. Eugene Jolas' "Manifesto: The Revolution of the Word" was adopted by Colin MacCabe as the title of his 1978 book *The Revolution of the Word*; Josiah Mitchell Morse wrote *Sympathetic Alien: James Joyce and Catholicism* in 1959; Kevin J. H. Dettmar's *The Illicit Joyce of Postmodernism: Reading Against the Grain* was published in 1996.

2. For an expanded treatment of this question, see the special issue of *Novel: A Forum on Fiction*, "Joyce and the Police," 29, no. 1 (fall 1995).

3. See Carol Schloss's "Joyce's Will," in *Novel* 29, no. 1 (fall 1995): 114–27.

4. This exchange took place at the 1996 International Joyce Symposium in Zurich, Switzerland. Paul Saint-Amour, then a graduate student at Stanford, had delivered a paper describing Samuel Roth's piracy as consonant with modernism's techniques of appropriation. In discussion afterward, he asked Joyce whether or not he thought his grandfather had been hypocritical. Given Stephen Joyce's jealous guarding of access to Joyce documents, this reply was a surprise.

5. Now, Joyce has himself been Bartletted, but clearly in reverence, not in ridicule. See Bernard McCabe's collection of quotations and Joycean maxims, *James Joyce: Reflections of Ireland*.

Chapter 4

1. It is clear here and elsewhere that I am following a reading of presence and absence in relation to the written that is articulated, on the one hand, in Walter Ong's *Orality and Literacy,* and on the other, in Jacques Derrida's *Of Grammatology.*

2. Seymour Chatman suggests the range of critical associations with the word "style." "'*What is style?*' As everyone knows, 'style' is an ambiguous term. Among other things, it has been used to refer to the idiosyncratic manner of an individual or group, or to a small-scale formal property of texts . . . ; or to a kind of extra or heightened expressiveness, present in nonliterary language as well; or to a decorum based on social or cultural context; or to any one of a number of other concepts." See *Literary Style: A Symposium,* xi.

3. See Brian Vickers's *In Defense of Rhetoric,* especially "The Three Styles," 80–82.

4. Once one begins to look, examples abound. The word "character" shares this etymology of a written thing being increasingly associated with the personal. The *Oxford English Dictionary* informs us that in the fourteenth century, a "character" is a written symbol. By the eighteenth century, it has come to mean a distinct personality in a written work.

5. Joyce touched friends for loans on the strength of his literary prospects. After showing those who counted as the literary establishment a few poems (George Russell, W. B. Yeats, Augusta Gregory), Joyce got them to lend him money and other forms of aid. Russell (A.E.) thought of him, not facetiously, as the "next generation [of writer]" (R. Ellmann, *Joyce,* 112).

6. Willard Potts, 1979.

7. See Chester Anderson's *James Joyce.* Its pictures document places explicitly mentioned in the books, captioning the sites with citations from Joyce's work. Anderson reads the works back into Joyce's life.

8. All *Portrait* review citations derive from *James Joyce: The Critical Heritage,* ed. Robert Deming, vol. 1.

9. Genesis depicts the two theories of language. God's word brings a reality into being out of nothingness, but then Adam begins attaching names to a preexistent reality. "And whatsoever Adam called every living creature, that was the name thereof" (Gen. 2:19). God, then, is a structuralist linguist, while Adam is of the old school.

10. Reading Stephen as symbol for Christ is standard enough practice for the approach to be listed under "Some Suggested Research Paper Topics" in *Portraits of an Artist,* an undergraduate compendium of *Portrait* criticism edited by William E. Morris and Clifford A. Nault. See also, in that collection, Chester Anderson's "The Sacrificial Butter," 267–77.

11. "Ulysses Gramophone: Hear Say Yes in Joyce," 35.

12. To the everlasting confusion of many points of his text. For instance, when Dennis Breen receives an anonymous postcard in the "Lestrygonians" episode of *Ulysses.* Mrs. Breen shows it to Bloom. "She took a folded postcard from her hand-

bag. —Read that, she said. He got it this morning. —What is it? Mr Bloom asked, taking the card. U.P.? —U.p.:up, she said. Someone taking a rise out of him. It's a great shame for them, whoever he is." (*U*, 8.255–59). Now what does the card say? "U.P.," or "U.P.:up"? Donald Gifford and Robert Seidman assume the latter (*"Ulysses" Annotated*, revised, 163), R. B. Kershner the former ("More Evidence on Breen's Telegram [*sic*]," *James Joyce Quarterly* 29, no. 2 [winter 1992]: 407–8). But on what grounds can we decide?

Chapter 5

1. Postmodernity is variously held as a new *episteme* (Arthur Kroker, Jean Baudrillard, Paul Virilo, Fredric Jameson), a new aesthetic (Rosalind Krauss, Brian Wallis) and a new politics (Francois Lyotard, P.M.) though the term "anti" or perhaps "non" might be affixed to each of these terms. See Hal Foster's introduction to *The Anti-Aesthetic*. One thing is for sure: postmodernity is a new subdiscipline of commodified knowledge within the modern academy of higher education.

2. Michael Allen Gillespie's 1984 *Hegel, Heidegger, and the Ground of History* echoes Fr. Gilbert Garraghan's 1940 *Guide to Historical Method* in striking this chord as a prelude. Gillespie takes up the question of historical representation in a sustained philosophical way, while Garraghan asks the question only to answer it swiftly and get on to the historical work at hand. More recent extended treatments include Peter Novick's *That Noble Dream: The "Objectivity Question" and the American Historical Profession* (New York: Cambridge University Press, 1988), and *Telling the Truth About History*, ed. Joyce Appleby, Lynn Hunt, and Margaret Jacob.

3. See E. H. Carr's 1961 Trevelyan Lectures, collected under the title *What Is History?* especially chapter 1, "The Historian and His Facts." Like Garraghan before him and Gillespie after, Carr is worried over the relative objectivity of historical reading. The more contemporary and general question of the impact of hermeneutics, structuralism, and poststructuralism on the discipline of history is considered in *Modern European Intellectual History*, edited by Dominick LaCapra and Steven L. Kaplan; also, LaCapra's *Rethinking Intellectual History: Texts, Contexts, Language* and *History and Criticism*. Also, Derek Attridge, Geoff Bennington, and Robert Young's *Post-Structuralism and the Question of History*. For an overview of the impact of poststructuralism on history (and a critique of LaCapra's work), see Anthony Pagden's "Rethinking the Linguistic Turn" or John E. Toews's "Intellectual History After the Linguistic Turn."

4. This point has a long history, from Platonic suspicion of mimesis and sophistry to an American insistence on plain talk. See Brian Vickers's *In Defense of Rhetoric*, or, more briefly, Ted Cohen's introduction "Metaphor and the Cultivation of Intimacy."

5. Outside of history proper, two tense locations for this issue are biblical hermeneutics and legal theory, especially with regard to the Supreme Court, where Justices are divided regarding the possibility of recouping the "original intent" of the United States Constitution.

6. For Ginzburg's more fully articulated approach, see his *Clues, Myths, and the*

Historical Method. For a critique of his method, see Dominick LaCapra's *History and Criticism*.

7. "It is Ginzburg's merit to have recognized . . . that—contrary to what has often been assumed—the documents of the Inquisition allow us to catch the voices of its victims and to reconstruct their intellectual universe, public and private. It takes a highly skilled and, above all, an imaginative historian to do so" (Hobsbaum, in Ginzburg, x). But how authentic could a modern imagination be?

8. Derrida's quotational strategies demonstrate the rhetorical dynamic of control I am describing. It is sometimes difficult to see Condillac beyond Derrida's powerful use of him. "Signature Event Context" evoked a reply from John Searle, and a further reply from Derrida, later published as *Limited, Inc*. In that piece, Derrida quotes the Searle essay bit by bit, until it is quite gone.

9. William York Tindall's phrase, from *Forces in Modern British Literature*, 21.

10. See, for instance, Michael Levenson's *A Genealogy of Modernism*, which sees the question of history as so thoroughly effaced both in the texts of modernism and in its criticism, that he intends to "help restore modernity to history" (Levenson, xi).

11. Robert Spoo's *James Joyce and the Language of History* reviews, through Stephen Dedalus, the young Joyce's disposition toward history, that "shout in the street," and that "nightmare from which I am trying to awake." One of the most significant services Spoo's excellent book does us is to return us to the metahistorical context in which Joyce wrote, a context of progressive, unified, history against which Joyce ranged his Nietzschean view.

12. See Norris's *The Decentered Universe of "Finnegans Wake"* and Kim Devlin's *Wandering and Return in "Finnegans Wake."*

13. Jean-Francois Lyotard, *The Postmodern Condition*.

14. I follow Diane Elam's assessment of postmodernity's relationship with history as ironic and uncertain, but hardly moot, as Griselda Pollock and others have claimed. See Elam's *Romancing the Postmodern*, 10–11.

Chapter 6

1. Bonnie Kime Scott makes just this point: "Her [Mrs. Dedalus's] threatening aspect after her death results from Stephen's guilt over using her life and from his unconscious projections" (*Joyce and Feminism*, 51).

2. "Joyce's female family were what Tillie Olsen calls 'silent' women . . . [they] left few recoverable traces" (*Joyce and Feminism*, 55).

3. Kevin Dettmar presented "Kathy Acker and Postmodern Appropriation" at University of California, Irvine, July 1, 1993, as part of the conference "California Joyce."

4. Joyce complained of the chaos in which he composed, contrasting it with Proust's soundproofed study. "Proust can write; he has a comfortable place at the Etoile, floored with cork and with cork on the walls to keep it quiet. And, I, writing in this place, people coming in and out. I wonder how I can finish *Ulysses*" (R. Ellmann, *Joyce*, 509). But it is hard to imagine his having begun *Ulysses* without all

those people, and what they had to say. By the time Joyce is writing *Finnegans Wake*, he can admit, "This book is being written by the people I have met or known" (Ellmann, *Joyce*, 6).

5. I follow this intertwining of the oral and the literate by way of characterization, but there are more purely textual markers at work as well. The much-discussed postcard received by Dennis Breen achieves its ambiguity by way of a slippage between the written and the spoken or thought. Bloom, shown the card, reads, "U.P:up." What does the card actually read, "U.P" or "U.P:up"? Beyond what the message in either form means, its exact written form, lost in the orality of its representation, is lost.

6. Jacques Derrida's *Of Grammatology* traces this tradition of the writtenness of the world, a tradition that has conflated the logocentric tradition of presence onto the written, so thinking of apprehending the world authentically as reading. Don Gifford reminds us that Stephen is quoting German mystic Jakob Boehme (1575–1624) and his *Signatura Rerum*.

7. Stuart Gilbert notes that the schema for *Ulysses* includes no emblematic organ for Stephen's chapters, the first three. Gilbert writes, "The explanation of this is probably that these episodes deal exclusively with the acts and thoughts of Stephen Dedalus, who, of the trinity of major personages appearing in *Ulysses* (Mr. Bloom, his wife, and Stephen), represents the spiritual element; in the same way, for the last episode, which is wholly devoted to the meditation of Marion Bloom (whose symbol is the Earth) there is no corresponding Art for she is a manifestation of Nature herself, the antithesis of art" (Gilbert, 30–31).

8. Joyce's men share with his women many of the hallmarks of orality. They are not readers (except of sporting sheets and newspapers), but their oral characteristics seem to mark vice rather than positive presence. "The Citizen" is most assuredly caught up in repetitive, conservative language that resists analysis or critique, but this is a sign of his ignorance and brutality. The scene at the newspaper in "Aeolus" stages male orality as blowsy rhetoric: hot air.

9. "Gabriel found himself partnered with Miss Ivors. She was a frank-mannered, talkative young lady, with a freckled face and prominent brown eyes. She did not wear a low-cut bodice and the large brooch which was fixed in the front of her collar bore on it an Irish device" (*Dubliners*, 213). Molly Ivors is generally positively depicted here, with the possible exception of the choice of the verb "bore" in the final sentence. Her intelligence is paired with her clear signal of sexual unavailability: she did not wear a low-cut bodice.

10. Morris Beja identifies this difference in Joyce's taste: that he rather liked women, but while in life the literary ones were his friends, publishers, and patrons (Marie Jolas, Sylvia Beach, Harriet Shaw Weaver), literate women do not figure positively in the works. See Beja, 21.

11. Woman as plagiarist is a figure that recurs both in *Ulysses* and in the Joyce biography. See my "Joyce and the Stakes of Style—or—the Case of the Copied Letter."

12. I hope I make clear here that I am not falling into the trap Elaine Unkeless has indicated, of viewing Molly's illiteracy, or perhaps we should say, her aliteracy, as a sign of her natural wisdom and superiority. I am interested in making clear a difference, not a hierarchy. See "The Conventional Molly Bloom," in *Women in Joyce*.

13. For a full history of women readers, see Kate Flint's *The Woman Reader 1837–1914*.

14. "Penelope" reveals that Molly has read *The Shadow of Ashlydyat* (1863) and *East Lynne* (1861), by Ellen (Mrs. Henry) Wood; *The Moonstone* (1868), by Wilkie Collins (and probably other works by Collins); *Henry Dunbar* (1864), by Mary Elizabeth Braddon (Mrs. John Maxwell); *The Trial and Life of Eugene Aram* (1832), by Edward Bulwer-Lytton; and *Molly Bawn* (1878), by Margaret Wolfe Hungerford. She has received, probably from Bloom, and has read, though with gaps of memory, Daniel Defoe's *Moll Flanders* (1772): "I dont like books with a Molly in them like that one he brought me about the one from Flanders a whore always shoplifting anything she could cloth and stuff and yards of it . . ." (*U*, 18.657–58). See Weldon Thornton's *Allusions in "Ulysses,"* 491–92.

15. *Sweets of Sin* recurs in verbatim or echoic form at 11.156, 11.692, 11.1106, 13.1196, 13.969, 13.1181, 15.297, 15.655, 15.1947, 15.3770, 16.1448 and 16.1468.

16. Lynda Nead has traced this containment of the body within the tradition of the nude in her *The Female Nude: Art, Obscenity, and Sexuality*, especially in "Aesthetics and the Female Nude," 22–25. From Descartes to Kant, the somatic or bodily response to the nude has been rigorously controlled and excluded by the concepts of critical objectivity, formal beauty, and the sublime.

Chapter 7

1. Harold Bloom's 1973 *Anxiety of Influence,* for a time itself a widely influential book, enscripts the problem: "How do men become poets, or to adopt older phrasing, how is the poetic character incarnated? When a potential poet first discovers (or is discovered by) the dialectic of influence, he first discovers poetry as being both external and internal to himself . . . the poet is condemned to learn his profoundest yearning through an awareness of *other selves*. The poem is *within* him, yet he experiences the shame and splendor of *being found by* poems—great poems—*outside* him. To lose freedom in this center is never to forgive, and to learn the dread of threatened autonomy forever" (Bloom, 25–26).

2. Leavis writes, "The student has to learn, as a matter of firm personal possession, the difference between real thinking and what ordinarily passes for that. It is a difficult and painful business. . . . The difficulty of learning what it is will elude his apprehension in the ardours and endurances, the confident new assaults on Everests of knowledge prescribed for him" (Leavis, 165). See also Terry Eagleton's description of Leavisian rigor: "Appalled by the complacent assumption that any work written in elegant English was more or less as good as any other, [Leavis's *Scrutiny*] insisted on the most rigorous discrimination between different literary qualities: some works 'made for life,' while others most assuredly did not" (Eagleton, 33).

3. See René Wellek and Austin Warren's *Theory of Literature:* "Even though 'reading' be used broadly enough to include critical understanding and sensibility, the art of reading is an ideal for a purely personal cultivation. As such it is highly desirable, and also serves as a basis of a widely spread literary culture. It cannot, however, replace the conception of 'literary scholarship,' conceived of as a superpersonal tradition, as a growing body of knowledge, insights, and judgements" (19).

4. See, for instance, Susan Sontag's "Against Interpretation" in *The Critical Tradition,* ed. David H. Richter, 545–50. For an example that predates Warren and Wellek, see D. H. Lawrence's 1928 essay on John Galsworthy, which dismisses objective interpretation with, "Literary criticism can be no more than a reasoned account of the feeling produced upon the critic by a book. Criticism can never be a science." Lawrence, of course, handed this sense of a *force* within reading on to his close reader, F. R. Leavis, who turned it into a "rigorous" critical distinction.

5. *Is There a Text in This Class?* (Cambridge: Harvard University Press, 1980).

6. In other places, Compagnon is clearly suspicious of means of textual control, such as a tendency toward definitional totality. In a brief article published much later (*La seconde main* is Compagnon's primary doctoral dissertation), Compagnon writes at what was then thought to be the verge of European unification: "I shall end here, insisting once again that though conscious of history—history, which I have not mentioned as perhaps the most perverse European invention—my overview is not historical. Europe is present everywhere yet invisible; the circumference is everywhere and the centre nowhere. We should be wary of a definition that makes it akin to God. That is why I have tried to map out the idea of Europe in such a pedestrian fashion." Compagnon will map, but from the ground, not from the air. See "Mapping the European Mind."

7. For a realignment of the subject/object split theorized through the act of reading, see Georges Poulet's "Criticism and the Experience of Interiority."

8. See Kenneth Burke, *A Grammar of Motives,* 512.

9. Joseph Blotner's mammoth biography of William Faulkner, for example, carefully traces the many specific and general influences of continental modernism on the writer, resident in Paris and reading voraciously at the outset of his career. But Blotner is careful to indicate a constant transmutation of source material at each point of influence. See Blotner, 549, 600–601.

10. Neither Lucia nor Nora Joyce spoke of Joyce as if he were dead. Richard Ellmann recounts how, when she was told the news of her father's death, Lucia asked, "What is he doing under the ground, that idiot? When will he decide to come out? He's watching us all the time." Nora Joyce, visiting Joyce's grave in Fluntern cemetery, near a zoo, would tell companions, "My husband is buried there. He was awfully fond of the lions—I like to think of him lying there and listening to them roar" (Ellmann, *Joyce,* 755–56).

11. Joseph Kelly traces this process of authorial effacement through the composition of the Ellmann biography in his useful article "Stanislaus Joyce, Ellsworth Mason, and Richard Ellmann: The Making of *James Joyce,*" 98–140.

12. Joyceans have begun to ask to what extent Ellmann's version of Joyce's life

has been personally influenced by another Joyce: Stanislaus. See Ira Nadel's "The Incomplete Joyce," 86–100; and Robert Spoo's comments in *James Joyce Quarterly* 29, no. 1 (fall 1991): 6–7.

13. Speaking of borrowings: Benstock's admission that the binary outsider/insider became muted and obscured, proximate to the name of Derrida, suggests that Derrida's textual presence touches off this particular derridean observation.

14. Kenner points out this kind of stylistic gravitation toward the object, a peculiar trick of Joyce's, in his *Joyce's Voices*. See the "Uncle Charles Principle," cited in chapter 2.

Bibliography

Acker, Kathy. *Great Expectations*. New York: Grove Press, 1982.
Adams, Hazard, and Leroy Searle, eds. *Critical Theory since 1965*. Tallahassee: Florida State University Press, 1986.
Algeo, John. *English: An Introduction to Language*. New York: Harcourt, Brace, and Jovanovich, 1968.
Anderson, Chester. *James Joyce*. London: Thames and Hudson, 1967.
———. "The Sacrificial Butter." In *Portraits of an Artist,* ed. William Morris and Clifford Nault. New York: Odyssey Press, 1962.
Appleby, Joyce, Lynn Hunt, and Margaret Jacob. *Telling the Truth about History.* New York: Norton, 1994.
Aristotle. *Politics and Poetics,* trans. Benjamin Jowett and Thomas Twining. New York: Viking, 1957.
Attridge, Derek, Geoff Bennington, and Robert Young. *Post-Structuralism and the Question of History.* Cambridge: Cambridge University Press, 1987.
Balaban, Oded. *Subject and Consciousness: A Philosophical Inquiry into Self-Consciousness.* Savage, Md.: Rowman and Littlefield, 1990.
Barthes, Roland. *Image, Music, Text,* trans. Stephen Heath. New York: Hill and Wang, 1977.
———. "La mort de l'auteur." *Manteia 5* (1968): 12–17.
———. *S/Z,* trans. Richard Miller. New York: Hill and Wang, 1974.
Bartholomae, David, and Anthony Petrosky. *Ways of Reading.* 3d ed. Boston: Bedford Books, 1993.
Bartlett, John. *Familiar Quotations.* 14th ed. Boston: Little, Brown and Co., 1968.
Beck, Emily Morison, ed. Preface to *Familiar Quotations.* 14th ed. Boston: Little, Brown and Co., 1968.
Beckett, Samuel. "Dante . . . Bruno, Vico . . . Joyce." In *Our Exagmination Round His Factification for Incamination of Work in Progress.* Paris: Shakespeare and Company, 1929.
Beja, Morris. *James Joyce: A Literary Life.* Columbus: Ohio State University Press, 1992.
Benjamin, Walter. *Illuminations,* ed. Hannah Arendt, trans. Harry Zohn. New York: Harcourt, Brace and World, 1968.
Benstock, Bernard. "The James Joyce Industry: An Assessment in the Sixties." *Southern Review* 2 (January 1966): 211–12.

Benstock, Shari. *Textualizing the Feminine: On the Limits of Genre.* Norman: Oklahoma Project for Discourse and Theory, 1991.

Birkett, Jennifer, and Elizabeth Harvey, eds. *Determined Women: Studies in the Construction of the Female Subject, 1900–1990.* London: Macmillan, 1991.

Birrell, Augustine. *Seven Lectures on the Law and History of Copyright in Books.* New York: Augustus M. Kelley, 1971.

Blamires, Harry. *The Bloomsday Book: A Guide Through Joyce's "Ulysses."* London: Methuen and Co., 1966.

Bloom, Harold. *The Anxiety of Influence.* London: Oxford University Press, 1973.

Blotner, Joseph. *Faulkner: A Biography.* New York: Random House, 1974.

Boller, Paul F. *Quotesmanship: The Use and Abuse of Quotations for Polemical and Other Purposes.* Dallas: Southern Methodist University Press, 1967.

Booker, M. Keith. *Joyce, Bakhtin, and the Literary Tradition.* Ann Arbor: University of Michigan Press, 1995.

Boswell, James. *The Life of Samuel Johnson.* New York: Doubleday, 1946.

Burgess, Anthony. *A Shorter "Finnegans Wake."* New York: Viking Press, 1968.

———. *Joycesprick.* London: Andre Deutsch, 1973.

Burke, Kenneth. *A Grammar of Motives.* New York: Prentice-Hall, 1945.

Cadava, Eduardo, Peter Connor, and Jean-Luc Nancy. *Who Comes After the Subject?* New York: Routledge, 1991.

Campbell, Joseph, and H. M. Robinson. *A Skeleton Key to "Finnegans Wake."* New York: Harcourt Brace, 1944.

Carr, E. H. *What Is History?* New York: Knopf, 1962.

Cascardi, Anthony. *The Subject of Modernity.* Cambridge: Cambridge University Press, 1992.

Chatman, Seymour. *Literary Style: A Symposium.* Oxford: Oxford University Press, 1971.

Chaucer, Geoffrey. *The Pardoners Prologue and Tale and The Shypmans Tale.* No press imprint, 1532. First edition in Arents Research Library, Syracuse, N.Y.

Chesterton, G. K. "The Wrong Shape." In *The Amazing Adventures of Father Brown.* New York: Dell Publishing, 1935.

Cixous, Helene. "The Laugh of the Medusa." In *Critical Theory since 1965,* ed. Hazard Adams and Leroy Searle. Tallahassee: Florida State University Press, 1986.

Cohen, Ted. "Metaphor and the Cultivation of Intimacy." *Critical Inquiry* 5, no. 1 (August 1978): 3–12.

Compagnon, Antoine. *La seconde main: ou, le travail de la citation.* Paris: Editions de Seuil, 1979.

———. "Mapping the European Mind." *Critical Quarterly* 32, no. 2 (Summer 1990): 1–7.

de Man, Paul. *Allegories of Reading.* New Haven: Yale University Press, 1977.

———. *The Resistance to Theory.* Minneapolis: University of Minnesota Press, 1986.

Deming, Robert H., ed. *James Joyce: The Critical Heritage.* vol. 1. New Haven: Yale University Press, 1971.

Dennison, Sally. *(Alternative) Literary Publishing*. Iowa City: University of Iowa Press, 1984.
Derrida, Jacques. *Of Grammatology*. Baltimore: Johns Hopkins University Press, 1974.
———. "Signature Event Context." In *Margins of Philosophy*, trans. Alan Bass. Chicago: University of Chicago Press, 1982.
———. "Ulysses Gramophone: Hear Say Yes in Joyce." In *The Augmented Ninth*, ed. Bernard Benstock. Syracuse: Syracuse University Press, 1988.
Dettmar, Kevin J. H. "Kathy Acker and Postmodern Appropriation." Unpublished paper delivered at "California Joyce," Conference at University of California at Irvine, July 1, 1993.
———. *The Illicit Joyce of Postmodernism: Reading Against the Grain*. Madison: University Press of Wisconsin, 1996.
———. *Marketing Modernisms: Self-Promotion, Canonization, Re-reading*. Ann Arbor: University of Michigan Press, 1996.
Devlin, Kimberly J. *Wandering and Return in "Finnegans Wake": An Integrative Approach to Joyce's Fiction*. Princeton: Princeton University Press, 1991.
Eagleton, Terry. *Literary Theory*. Oxford: Basil Blackwell, 1983.
Eisenstein, Elizabeth. *The Printing Press as an Agent of Change*. Vol. 2. Cambridge: Cambridge University Press, 1979.
———. *The Print Revolution in Early Modern Europe*. Cambridge: Cambridge University Press, 1983.
Elam, Diane. *Romancing the Postmodern*. London: Routledge, 1992.
Ellmann, Maud. *The Poetics of Impersonality*. Cambridge: Harvard University Press, 1987.
Ellmann, Richard. *The Consciousness of James Joyce*. Oxford: Oxford University Press, 1977.
———. *James Joyce*. New York: Oxford University Press, 1959.
Ellmann, Richard, with Charles Feidelson, Jr. *The Modern Tradition*. Oxford: Oxford University Press, 1965.
Fairhall, James. *James Joyce and the Question of History*. Cambridge: Cambridge University Press, 1993.
Fitzpatrick, David. "'A Share of the Honeycomb': Education, Emigration, and Irishwomen." In *The Origins of Popular Literacy in Ireland: Language, Change, and Educational Development 1700–1920*, ed. Mary Daly and David Dickson. Dublin: Department of Modern History, Trinity College, and Department of Modern Irish History, University College, 1990.
Flint, Kate. *The Woman Reader: 1837–1914*. Oxford: Clarendon Press, 1993.
Foster, Hal, ed. *The Anti-Aesthetic: Essays on Postmodern Culture*. Port Townsend, Wash.: Bay Press, 1983.
Foster, John. *A Shakespeare Word Book*. London: Russel and Russel, 1908.
Foucault, Michel. *The Archaeology of Knowledge and the Discourse on Language*, trans. A. M. Sheridan Smith. New York: Pantheon Books, 1972.
———. *Language, Countermemory, Practice: Selected Essays and Interviews*, trans. Donald F. Bouchard and Sherry Simon. Ithaca: Cornell University Press, 1977.

Fuss, Diana. *Essentially Speaking: Feminism, Nature, and Difference.* London: Routledge, 1989.
Genette, Gerard. *Palimpsests: la littérature au second degré.* Paris: Editions du Seuil, 1982.
Gilbert, Sandra. "Literary Paternity." In *Critical Theory since 1965,* ed. Hazard Adams and Leroy Searle. Tallahassee: Florida State University Press, 1986.
Gilbert, Stuart. *James Joyce's "Ulysses."* New York: Vintage Books, 1955.
Gillespie, Michael Allen. *Hegel, Heidegger, and the Ground of History.* Chicago: University of Chicago Press, 1984.
Ginzburg, Carlo. *Clues, Myths, and the Historical Method.* Baltimore: Johns Hopkins University Press, 1989.
———. *The Night Battles: Witchcraft and Agrarian Cults in the Sixteenth and Seventeenth Centuries,* trans. John and Anne Tedeschi. New York: Penguin Books, 1983. (First published in Italian in 1966.)
Godzich, Wlad, and Jeffrey Kittay. *The Emergence of Prose.* Ann Arbor: University of Michigan Press, 1987.
Gordon, John. *"Finnegans Wake": A Plot Summary.* Syracuse: Syracuse University Press, 1986.
Groden, Michael. "'Foostering Over Those Changes': The New *Ulysses.*" *James Joyce Quarterly* 22, no.2 (Winter 1985): 152.
Guskey, Thomas R. *Implementing Mastery Learning.* Belmont, Calif.: Wadsworth Publishing, 1985.
Havelock, Eric. *The Muse Learns to Write: Reflections on Orality and Literacy from Antiquity to the Present.* New Haven: Yale University Press, 1986.
Hebel, Udo. *Intertextuality, Allusion, and Quotation: An International Bibliography of Critical Studies.* Westport, Conn.: Greenwood Press, 1989.
Henriques, Julian, et al. *Changing the Subject: Psychology, Social Regulation, and Subjectivity.* London: Methuen, 1984.
Hollander, John. *The Figure of the Echo: A Mode of Allusion in Milton and After.* Berkeley: University of California Press, 1981.
Holman, Hugh. *A Handbook to Literature.* 3d ed. Indianapolis: Bobbs-Merrill, 1972.
Irigaray, Luce. "When Our Lips Speak Together." In *This Sex Which Is Not One,* trans. Catherine Porter. Ithaca: Cornell University Press, 1985.
Johnson, Samuel. Preface to the Dictionary. In *Samuel Johnson's Literary Criticism,* ed. R. D. Stock. Lincoln: University of Nebraska Press, 1974.
Johnston, Denis. "God's Gift to English Departments." *CEA Critic* 14, no. 2 (February 1952): 4–5.
Joyce, James. *A Portrait of the Artist as a Young Man.* New York: Penguin Books, 1985.
———. *Collected Letters of James Joyce,* ed. Richard Ellmann. New York: Viking Press, 1966.
———. *Dubliners.* New York: Penguin Books, 1967.
———. *Finnegans Wake.* New York: Viking Press, 1986.
———. *Ulysses,* ed. Hans Gabler. New York: Vintage Books, 1986.

Kant, Immanuel. "What is Enlightenment?" In *Foundations of the Metaphysics of Morals,* trans. Lewis White Beck. New York: Bobbs Merrill, 1959.
Kaufmann, Patrick. *Textual Bodies: Modernism, Postmodernism, and Print.* Lewisburg, Penn.: Bucknell University Press, 1994.
Kelly, Joseph. "Stanislaus Joyce, Ellsworth Mason, and Richard Ellmann: The Making of *James Joyce.*" In *Joyce Studies Annual.* Austin: University of Texas Press, 1992.
Kenner, Hugh. "The Joycean Present." *James Joyce Quarterly* 28, no. 4 (Summer 1991): 853–56.
———. *Joyce's Voices.* Berkeley: University of California Press, 1978.
———. *The Pound Era.* London: Faber and Faber, 1972.
———. *"Ulysses."* London: Allen and Unwin, 1980.
Koestenbaum, Wayne. *Doubletalk: The Erotics of Male Literary Collaboration.* New York: Routledge, 1989.
Knowlton, Barry. "Reading the Writing of Speeches." Unpublished paper, 1989.
Knowlton, Eloise. "Joyce and the Stakes of Style—or—the Case of the Copied Letter." *Style* 27, no. 1 (Spring 1993): 81–90.
Kolb, David. *Critique of Pure Modernity: Hegel, Heidegger, and After.* Chicago: Chicago University Press, 1986.
Krauss, Rosalind E. *The Originality of the Avant-Garde and Other Modernist Myths.* Cambridge: Massachusetts Institute of Technology Press, 1985.
LaCapra, Dominick. *History and Criticism.* Ithaca: Cornell University Press, 1985.
———. *Rethinking Intellectual History: Texts, Contexts, Language.* Ithaca: Cornell University Press, 1983.
LaCapra, Dominick, and Steven L. Kaplan, eds. *Modern European Intellectual History.* Ithaca: Cornell University Press, 1982.
Leavis, F. R. *The Critic as Anti-Philosopher: Essays and Papers,* ed. G. Singh. Athens: University of Georgia Press, 1983.
Leckie, Barbara. "'A Race of Angels': Postcolonialism and Pornography in Ulysses." Unpublished conference paper, delivered June 14, 1994, at "Transcultural Joyce," in Seville, Spain.
Lentz, Tony. *Orality and Literacy in Hellenic Greece.* Carbondale: Southern Illinois Press, 1989.
Lernout, Geert. *The French Joyce.* Ann Arbor: University of Michigan Press, 1990.
Levenson, Michael H. *A Genealogy of Modernism.* Cambridge: Cambridge University Press, 1984.
Lidderdale, Jane, and Mary Nicholson. *Dear Miss Weaver: Harriet Shaw Weaver.* London: Faber, 1970.
Lyotard, Jean-François. *The postmodern Condition: A Report on Knowledge.* Minneapolis: University of Minnesota Press, 1984.
MacCabe, Bernard. *James Joyce: Reflections of Ireland.* New York: Macmillan, 1993.
MacCabe, Colin. *The Revolution of the Word.* London: MacMillan, 1978.
Maddox, Brenda. *Nora: A Biography of Nora Joyce.* London: Minerva, 1986.
Mallon, Thomas. *Stolen Words: Forays in the Origins and Ravages of Plagiarism.* New York: Tickner and Fields, 1989.

Marshall, Donald. Introduction to *Philosophy Beside Itself*, by Stephen Melville. Minneapolis: University of Minnesota Press, 1986.
McCabe, Bernard, ed. *James Joyce: Reflections of Ireland*. New York: Macmillan, 1993.
McCarthy, Patrick, ed. *Critical Essays on James Joyce's "Finnegans Wake."* New York: G. K. Hall, 1992.
McCrillis, John O. C. *Printers' Abecedarium*. Boston: Godine, 1974.
McDowell, Lesley, and Catherine Driscoll, eds. *Joyce's Daughters*. Cambridge: Cambridge University Press, forthcoming 1998.
McHugh, Roland. *Annotations to "Finnegans Wake."* Baltimore: Johns Hopkins University Press, 1980.
———. *The "Finnegans Wake" Experience*. Berkeley: University of Calfornia Press, 1981.
McQuade, Donald, and Robert Atwan, eds. *Thinking in Writing*. 3d ed. New York: Knopf, 1988.
Meisel, Perry. *The Myth of the Modern*. New Haven: Yale University Press, 1987.
Merton, Thomas. *On the Shoulders of Giants: A Shandean Perspective*. New York: Free Press, 1965.
Meyer, Herman. *The Poetics of Quotation in the European Novel*, trans. Theodore and Yetta Ziolkowski. Princeton: Princeton University Press, 1968.
Milton, John. *History of Britain*. 1670. First edition in George Arents Research Library, Syracuse, N.Y.
Moi, Toril. *Sexual/Textual Politics: Feminist Literary Theory*. London: Routledge, 1989.
Montaigne, Michel de. *Essayes*, trans. John Florio. London: Val Sims for Edward Blount, 1603. First edition in George Arents Research Library, Syracuse, N.Y.
Morris, William E., and Clifford A. Nault, Jr., eds. *Portraits of an Artist: A Casebook*. New York: Odyssey Press, 1962.
Morse, Josiah Mitchell. *Sympathetic Alien: James Joyce and Catholicism*. New York: New York University Press, 1959.
Murray's English Grammar. Hartford: Peter Gleason and Co., 1813.
Nadel, Ira. "The Incomplete Joyce." In *Joyce Studies Annual*. Austin: University of Texas Press, 1991.
Nead, Lynda. *The Female Nude: Art, Obscenity, and Sexuality*. London: Routledge, 1992.
Norris, Margot. *The Decentered Universe of "Finnegans Wake": A Structuralist Analysis*. Baltimore: Johns Hopkins Press, 1974.
———. *Penelope's Web: The Social Unraveling of Modernism*. Austin: University of Texas Press, 1992.
Ong, Walter. *Orality and Literacy: The Technologizing of the Word*. London: Routledge, 1982.
Pagden, Anthony. "Rethinking the Linguistic Turn: Current Anxieties in Intellectual History." *Journal of the History of Ideas* 49 (July/September 1988): 519–29.
Parkes, M. B. *Pause and Effect: An Introduction to the History of Punctuation in the West*. Berkeley: University of California Press, 1992.

Pater, Walter. "Style." In *Norton Anthology of English Literature*. 5th ed., vol. 2. New York: Norton, 1986.

Poulet, Georges. "Criticism and the Experience of Interiority." In *The Structuralist Controversy: The Languages of Criticism and the Sciences of Man*, ed. Richard Macksey and Eugenio Donato. Baltimore: Johns Hopkins Press, 1970.

Pucci, Pietro. *Odysseus Polutropos: Intertextual Readings in the "Odyssey" and the "Iliad."* Ithaca: Cornell University Press, 1987.

Ransom, Harry. *The First Copyright Statute*. Austin: University of Texas Press, 1956.

Richter, David H., ed. *The Critical Tradition*. New York: St. Martin's Press, 1989.

Rigg, A. G. *The English Language*. New York: Appleton, Century, and Crofts, 1968.

Rose, Mark. *Authors and Owners: The Invention of Copyright*. Cambridge: Harvard University Press, 1993.

Sartiliot, Claudette. *Citation and Modernity: Derrida, Joyce, and Brecht*. Norman: Oklahoma University Press, 1993.

Satamurti, Carole. *Changing the Subject*. Oxford: Oxford University Press, 1990.

Schloss, Carol. "Joyce's Will." *Novel* 29, no. 1 (Fall 1995).

Scott, Bonnie Kime. *Joyce and Feminism*. Bloomington: Indiana University Press, 1984.

———. *Refiguring Modernism*. Bloomington: Indiana University Press, 1996.

Smith, Paul. *Discerning the Subject*. Minneapolis: University of Minnesota Press, 1988.

Speilburg, Peter. "Take a Shaggy Dog by the Tale." *James Joyce Quarterly* 1, no. 3 (Spring 1964): 42–46.

Spellmeyer, Kurt. "The Essay in the Academy." *College English* 51, no. 3 (March 1989): 262–75.

Spoo, Robert. *James Joyce and the Language of History*. Oxford: Oxford University Press, 1994.

Tanner, Stephen. "Joyce and Modern Critical Theory." *Arizona Quarterly* 40 (Autumn 1984): 269–79.

Taylor, Charles. *The Ethics of Authenticity*. Cambridge: Harvard University Press, 1991.

———. *Sources of the Self: The Making of the Modern Identity*. Cambridge: Harvard University Press, 1989.

Thornton, Weldon. *Allusions in "Ulysses."* Chapel Hill: University of North Carolina Press, 1961.

Tindall, William York. *Forces in Modern British Literature 1885–1946*. New York: A. A. Knopf, 1947.

Topia, André. "The Matrix and the Echo: Intertextuality in *Ulysses*." *The Post-Structuralist Joyce*, ed. Derek Attridge and Daniel Ferrer. Cambridge: Cambridge University Press, 1984.

Toews, John E. "Intellectual History After the Linguistic Turn: The Autonomy of Meaning and the Irreducibility of Experience." *American Historical Review* 92 (October 1987): 879–907.

Unkeless, Elaine. "The Conventional Molly Bloom." In *Women in Joyce*. Urbana: University of Illinois Press, 1982.

Vickers, Brian. *In Defense of Rhetoric*. Oxford: Clarendon Press, 1988.

Vonnegut, Kurt. "How to Write with Style." In *Thinking in Writing*, ed. Donald McQuade and Robert Atwan. New York: Knopf, 1988.

Weedon, Chris. *Feminist Practice and Post-Structuralist Theory*. Oxford: Basil Blackwell, 1987.

Wellek, René, and Austin Warren. *Theory of Literature*. San Diego: Harcourt Brace Jovanovich, 1977.

White, Hayden. *Metahistory: The Historical Imagination in Nineteenth-Century Europe*. Baltimore: Johns Hopkins University Press, 1973.

Whorf, Benjamin Lee. *Language, Thought, Reality*. Cambridge: Cambridge University Press, 1956.

Wilde, Oscar. *The Artist as Critic*. Richard Ellmann, ed. Chicago: University of Chicago Press, 1968.

Index

Acker, Kathy, 85
Adams, Hazard, 19, 116
A.E. (George Russell), 118
Anderson, Chester, 118
A Portrait of the Artist as a Young Man, 2, 43–46, 53–59, 82, 84, 108, 110
Appleby, Joyce, 119
Aristotle, 38, 45, 52
Arnold, Matthew, 106
Attridge, Derek, 119
auctoritas, 40–43
Augustine, 25, 116
author, 53–58

Bainton, Roland, 116
Barnacle, Nora, 35–36, 95, 123
Barthes, Roland, 18, 83, 103
Bartholomae, David, 102
Bartlett's Familiar Quotations, 117
Beckett, Samuel, 6, 11, 106
Beja, Morris, 121
Benjamin, Walter, 116
Bennington, Geoffrey, 119
Benstock, Bernard, 109–10, 124
Benveniste, Emile, 18
Birkett, Jennifer, 116
Birrell, Augustine, 24
Blamires, Harry, 6
Bloom, Harold, 122
Blotner, Joseph, 123
Boller, Paul, 115
Booker, M. Keith, 115
Borges, Jorge Luis, 86
Boswell, James, 102
Brion, Marcel, 76
Budgen, Frank, 38

Burgess, Anthony, 3
Burke, Kenneth, 17, 123

Cadava, Edward, 19, 116
Campbell, Joseph, 3–7
Carr, E. H., 69–70, 119
Carr, Henry, 35
Cascardi, Anthony, 116
Chatman, Seymour, 118
Chaucer, Geoffrey, 29
citation: and quotation, difference between, 9; modernist, 73–78; postmodern, 112–13
Cohen, Ted, 119
Compagnon, Antoine, 9, 16–17, 18, 20, 26, 104, 115, 123
Condillac. 72
Connor, Peter, 116

de Man, Paul, 104
Deming, Robert, 107, 118
Derrida, Jacques, 60, 71–73, 76, 78, 85, 89, 104, 107, 118, 120, 121, 124
Dettmar, Kevin J. H., 35, 86, 117, 120
Devlin, Kim, 76, 120
Dickens, Charles, 85
Driscoll, Catherine, 63
Dubliners, 2, 39–43

Eagleton, Terry, 122
Eisenstein, Elizabeth, 117
Eliot, T. S., 39, 52, 74, 110, 116
Elam, Diane, 120
Ellmann, Maud, 116
Ellmann, Richard: *Consciousness of Joyce,* 61–62; *James Joyce,* 2, 35–36, 38, 75, 77–78, 108–9; *Modern Tradition,* 65

Fairhall, James, 76
Faulkner, William, 106
Fiedelson, Charles, 65
Finnegans Wake, 2, 3–8, 10–11, 75–78
Fitzpatrick, David, 93
Flanagan, Fionulla, 90
Flint, Kate, 98, 116, 122
Foster, Hal, 65
Foucault, Michel, 8–9, 18, 37, 107
Frobens brothers, 27

Garraghan, Gilbert, 119
Genesis, 118
Genette, Gerard, 115
Gifford, Donald, 46, 97, 119
Gilbert, Sandra, 25, 85
Gilbert, Stuart, 121
Gillespie, Michael Allen, 119
Ginzburg, Carlo, 67–68, 119, 120
God, a structuralist, 118
Gordon, John, 3
Gorman, Herbert, 109
Gregory, Augusta, 39, 118
Gubar, Susan, 25, 85

Hannibal, 27
Harvey, Elizabeth, 116
Henriques, Julian, 116
Hobsbaum, E. J., 67
Homer, 21, 26, 75
Hunt, Lynn, 119

Ibsen, Henrik, 39, 82–83, 110
Irigaray, Luce, 85
irony, 17. *See also* Burke, Kenneth

Jacob, Margaret, 119
James Joyce Quarterly, 62, 108
Jesus, 21, 40, 44
Johnson, Samuel, 103, 115
Jolas, Eugene, 35, 117
Joyce, James: and copyright, 24, 35–36; and history, 75–78; and quotation marks, 2, 60; and reading, 37–39
Joyce, Lucia, 123
Joyce, Michael, 36
Joyce, Stephen James, 36, 117
Joyceans, 35, 38–39, 46, 61, 106–13

Kant, Emmanuel, 5
Kaplan, Steven L., 119
Kelly, Joseph, 123
Kenner, Hugh, 58–59, 74–75, 90, 111–13, 124
Kershner, Brandon, 39, 119
Knowlton, Barry, 27
Koestenbaum, Wayne, 18
Krauss, Rosalind, 116
Kruger, Barbara, 86
Kuhn, Thomas, 107

Lacapra, Dominick, 119
Lawrence, D. H., 123
Lawrence, Karen, 62
Leavis, F. R., 102, 122
Lentz, Tony, 26
Lernout, Geert, 107–8
Levenson, Michael, 120
Levin, Harry, 108
Levy-Bruhl, Lucien, 87
Lewis, Wyndham, 74
Lyotard, Jean-Francois, 120

MacCabe, Colin, 35, 117
Mallon, Thomas, 23–24, 115, 117. *See also* plagiarism
Manutius, Aldus, 27
Mapplethorpe, Robert, 99
Marshall, Donald, 74, 110
McCabe, Bernard, 117
McDowell, Leslie, 63
McHugh, Roland, 3–4
Meese Committee, 99
Meisel, Perry, 64
Memorabilia, 38, 43
memorization, 22
Meyer, Herbert, 115
Milton, John, 31–33
Montaigne, Michel de, 15, 29–31
Morris, William E., 118
Morse, Josiah Mitchell, 35, 117

Nancy, Jean-Luc, 116
Nault, Clifford, 118
Nead, Lynda, 122
Norris, Margot, 24, 62, 76, 116, 120
Novick, Peter, 119

Pater, Walter. "Style." In *Norton Anthology of English Literature.* 5th ed., vol. 2. New York: Norton, 1986.

Poulet, Georges. "Criticism and the Experience of Interiority." In *The Structuralist Controversy: The Languages of Criticism and the Sciences of Man,* ed. Richard Macksey and Eugenio Donato. Baltimore: Johns Hopkins Press, 1970.

Pucci, Pietro. *Odysseus Polutropos: Intertextual Readings in the "Odyssey" and the "Iliad."* Ithaca: Cornell University Press, 1987.

Ransom, Harry. *The First Copyright Statute.* Austin: University of Texas Press, 1956.

Richter, David H., ed. *The Critical Tradition.* New York: St. Martin's Press, 1989.

Rigg, A. G. *The English Language.* New York: Appleton, Century, and Crofts, 1968.

Rose, Mark. *Authors and Owners: The Invention of Copyright.* Cambridge: Harvard University Press, 1993.

Sartiliot, Claudette. *Citation and Modernity: Derrida, Joyce, and Brecht.* Norman: Oklahoma University Press, 1993.

Satamurti, Carole. *Changing the Subject.* Oxford: Oxford University Press, 1990.

Schloss, Carol. "Joyce's Will." *Novel* 29, no. 1 (Fall 1995).

Scott, Bonnie Kime. *Joyce and Feminism.* Bloomington: Indiana University Press, 1984.

———. *Refiguring Modernism.* Bloomington: Indiana University Press, 1996.

Smith, Paul. *Discerning the Subject.* Minneapolis: University of Minnesota Press, 1988.

Speilburg, Peter. "Take a Shaggy Dog by the Tale." *James Joyce Quarterly* 1, no. 3 (Spring 1964): 42–46.

Spellmeyer, Kurt. "The Essay in the Academy." *College English* 51, no. 3 (March 1989): 262–75.

Spoo, Robert. *James Joyce and the Language of History.* Oxford: Oxford University Press, 1994.

Tanner, Stephen. "Joyce and Modern Critical Theory." *Arizona Quarterly* 40 (Autumn 1984): 269–79.

Taylor, Charles. *The Ethics of Authenticity.* Cambridge: Harvard University Press, 1991.

———. *Sources of the Self: The Making of the Modern Identity.* Cambridge: Harvard University Press, 1989.

Thornton, Weldon. *Allusions in "Ulysses."* Chapel Hill: University of North Carolina Press, 1961.

Tindall, William York. *Forces in Modern British Literature 1885–1946.* New York: A. A. Knopf, 1947.

Topia, André. "The Matrix and the Echo: Intertextuality in *Ulysses.*" *The Post-Structuralist Joyce,* ed. Derek Attridge and Daniel Ferrer. Cambridge: Cambridge University Press, 1984.

Toews, John E. "Intellectual History After the Linguistic Turn: The Autonomy of Meaning and the Irreducibility of Experience." *American Historical Review* 92 (October 1987): 879–907.

Unkeless, Elaine. "The Conventional Molly Bloom." In *Women in Joyce*. Urbana: University of Illinois Press, 1982.

Vickers, Brian. *In Defense of Rhetoric*. Oxford: Clarendon Press, 1988.

Vonnegut, Kurt. "How to Write with Style." In *Thinking in Writing,* ed. Donald McQuade and Robert Atwan. New York: Knopf, 1988.

Weedon, Chris. *Feminist Practice and Post-Structuralist Theory.* Oxford: Basil Blackwell, 1987.

Wellek, René, and Austin Warren. *Theory of Literature*. San Diego: Harcourt Brace Jovanovich, 1977.

White, Hayden. *Metahistory: The Historical Imagination in Nineteenth-Century Europe*. Baltimore: Johns Hopkins University Press, 1973.

Whorf, Benjamin Lee. *Language, Thought, Reality*. Cambridge: Cambridge University Press, 1956.

Wilde, Oscar. *The Artist as Critic*. Richard Ellmann, ed. Chicago: University of Chicago Press, 1968.

O'Brien, Flann, 106
Ong, Walter, 87–90, 117, 118
orality, 86–90
Ovid, 43

Pagden, Anthony, 119
Parkes, M. B., 25–26
Pater, Walter, 53
Petrosky, Anthony, 102
plagiarism, 23, 86, 121. *See also* Mallon, Thomas
Plato/Socrates, 26
postmodernity, 65, 112–13, 74–75, 86; and literacy 106
Potts, Willard, 118
Poulet, Georges, 123
Pound, Ezra, 52, 74, 116
Proust, Marcel, 120
punctuation. *See* quotation marks

quotation, history of, 19–27
quotation marks, 1, 18, 25–33
quotes, scare, 17

Ransom, Harry, 116
reading, Molly Bloom's, 122
Richards, Grant, 2
Rigg, A. G., 117
Robinson, H. M., 3–7
Rose, Mark, 24
Roth, Samuel, 36, 117. *See also* plagiarism
Rouse, Mary A., 116
Rouse, Richard H., 116
Russell, George (A.E.), 118

Said, Edward, 18
Saint-Amour, Paul, 117
Sapir, Edward, 18
Sartiliot, Claudette, 9, 113
Satamurti, Carole, 116
Satan, 21
Schloss, Carol, 117
Scott, Bonnie Kime, 39
Searle, John, 120

Searle, Leroy, 116
Seidman, Robert, 46, 119
Shakespeare, William, 19, 107, 116
Smith, Paul, 116
Socrates/Plato, 26
Sontag, Susan, 123
Speilburg, Peter, 108
Spellmeyer, Kurt, 16, 115
Spoo, Robert, 76, 120, 124
Stephen Hero, 82–84
Stoppard, Tom, 86
Sterne, Laurence, 78
style and quotation, 51–53
subjectivity, 8–11, 15–19
Synge, John, 38–39

Thornton, Weldon, 46, 122
Tindall, William York, 120
Toews, John, 119
Topia, Andre, 37, 46
Twine, Nanette, 117

Ulysses, 46–47, 60, 75, 81–82, 90–100, 108; Roth piracy of, 36
Unkeless, Elaine, 122

Vickers, Brian, 118, 119
Vico, Giambattista, 75
Vonnegut, Kurt, 51

Warhol, Andy, 86
Warren, Austin, 106–7, 123
Weaver, Harriet, 62, 77
Wellek, Rene, 106–7, 123
White, Hayden, 65–66
Whorf, Benjamin Lee, 18
Wilde, Oscar, 53
Wilson, Edmund, 111
Wittenstein, Ludwig, 107
Wodehouse, P. G., 102
Woolf, Virginia, 52

Yeats, W. B., 74–75, 82, 111, 118
Young, Robert, 119

Eloise Knowlton is assistant professor of humanities at Boston University. She has published essays in *Style, Children's Literature Association Quarterly,* and in the anthology *Rereading the New,* edited by Kevin J. H. Dettmar (Ann Arbor: University of Michigan Press, 1992).